OVERLAND TO CALIFORNIA — 1850

JOURNAL
OF
EDMUND CAVILEER HINDE

EDITED BY
JEROME PELTIER

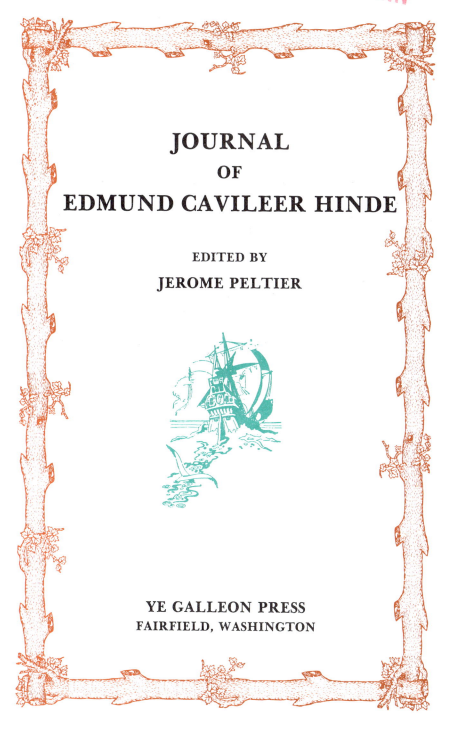

YE GALLEON PRESS
FAIRFIELD, WASHINGTON

Library of Congress Cataloging in Publication Data

Hinde, Edmund Cavileer, 1830-1909.
   Journal of Edmund Cavileer Hinde.

   Bibliography: p.
   Includes index.
   1. Overland journeys to the Pacific. 2. West (U.S.)—Description and
travel—1848-1860. 3. Hinde, Edmund Cavileer, 1830-1909. I Peltier,
Jerome. II. Title.
F593.H56   1983   917.8'042   83-23398
ISBN 0-87770-313-2

TABLE OF CONTENTS

ACKNOWLEDGEMENTS

I wish to express my appreciation for aid that was given to me in the production of this book.

First and foremost I wish to thank Glen Adams and his most capable staff for its typographical excellence and the entire design of the book.

I wish to give special thanks to the California Historical Society of San Francisco, California and in particular to Joy Berry, its reference librarian for aid in locating some of the places mentioned in the diary that I had difficulty in identifying.

I also wish to acknowledge the services rendered by Mr. and Mrs. Harold Wright of Spokane, Washington.

Thanks also to Welch-Ryce Association of Santa Barbara, California for furnishing a copy of certificate of death of Edmund Hinde.

Thanks to Carolyn Grannar for typing the manuscript from my longhand notes, a difficult job at best.

A blanket "thank you" to all those authors whose books I used as reference tools while at work on this book.

Special thanks are due to my wonderful wife whose patience and forebearance while I was at work on the manuscript was most notable.

I received indifferent responses when I asked for aid and verification regarding the New Orleans part of Hinde's journal but I do wish to thank the *New Orleans Picayune* newspaper people and the staff of the public library for at least answering my letters.

If I have forgotten to mention anyone else who helped me it is unintentional and I hope that he or she will accept my humble apologies.

Jerome Peltier

INTRODUCTION

Little is known about the writer of this journal other than that which he tells us about himself and from his death certificate. Edmund Cavileer Hinde was born April 6, 1830 in Urbana, Ohio. His father was Thomas S. Hinde of the above-named city. His mother a native of Charleston, Maryland was named Sarah O. Cavileer. This data was given by Harry H. Hinde, a son of Edmund, at the time of his death, December 20, 1909 in Riverside, California.

Edmund's diary begins abruptly on September 10, 1849 at Mt. Carmel, Illinois. It commences on a very pessimistic note and continues in that vein until September 24th at which time he informs us that he will journey to St. Louis, Missouri in search of work in just a week.

Edmund Hinde informs us that he is an orphan and at different times he names his brothers and sisters in his diary entries, so that we are enabled to piece together at least a part of his family history. On September 28th he wrote a letter to his fourteen-year-old sister who lived with an uncle in Springfield, Ohio. From this entry it would appear that members of his family were farmed out to relatives, if under working age, or left to their own devices, as our nineteen-year-old diarist was, if of a working age. It would appear also that Edmund had promised to care for this younger sister until she "will not require my assistance."

In an early entry and just before he left for St. Louis Edmund visited the graves of his parents.

As far as I have been able to ascertain, Edmund had two sisters Martha and Bellinda and either two or three brothers, John M. Hinde, Charles T. Hinde and Matt Hinde. The reason why I say two or three brothers is because Matt might be the middle name of John *M*. I do not know whether Martha or Bellinda was the 14-year-old to whom he wrote before leaving for St. Louis.

He planned to travel with a group of delegates to what he called the "Hillsboro convention a state policy convention." The first night of the trip brought them five miles short of Maysville. The next day he visited his brother J.M. Hinde in that town after which he proceeded to Jeralls (?) and from there to Vandalia and on to Hillsboro. He returned to Vandalia and eventually reached St. Louis on October 6, 1849.

While in St. Louis he spent several days in a fruitless search for work On October 9th he was offered a job by a saddle maker but did not seem to be pleased with the prospects because it would take him to the small town of Madisonville, Ralls County, Missouri which lay about 120 miles north of St. Louis.

He "tossed his cap" to decide whether he would accept the saddler's job or move on up to Minnesota Territory and search for work there. Two of three flips of his cap decided his next move which was to take the Madisonville job.

In the above community he worked as a saddle and harness maker for H.P. Haley until the gold fever struck him the following spring, at which time our journal begins.

Jerome Peltier

Wherever possible, original spelling and punctuation was followed.

Overland to California — 1850

March 5th — For the last month I have neglected to keep any account of what has transpired. The California fever still rages at the highest pitch. I am its victim and have wrote to all of my friends and informed them of my intentions.

Mr. Haley[1] left for St. Louis yesterday to select all such articles we needed for the trip.

Tomorrow is our mail day and I hope to get some news as well as some assistance. I have not heard from home for sometime and if some of them do[es] not aid me I will be flat soon.

March 17. Sunday Evening. — I have been so dambedly taken off with the California fever that I have neglected the book which was once a pleasure to me when the Blue Devils was on me. On last monday week the 6th of this month I received fowling [*sic* following] letters one from Jno M.[2] Chas F.[3] and Bell Hinde[4] one from Martha[5] one from Charles H.[6] who by some fortunate means sent me $50. which is all I looked for from him for which I thank him kindly.

March 24 — All the nois [*sic*] stir and confusion is about California and Trains are continually pouring through here[7] on their way. On last wednesday I received a letter from Charles T. I have sent for a small book to keep a memorandum of some of our scenes on the road. We are now making all the preparations necessary as speedy as possibly can be done. There was quite a fall of snow today but cleared off in the afternoon — I wrote a letter to my sister in Springfield but failed to send it so I will add more and send it on next Wednesday.[8]

March 30 — Monday eve. and tomorrow I open a new book and am determined to keep it correct.

Madisonville Ralls Co. Mo. March 31st/50 — In This book I intend to keep a record to my trip on the road to California as minutely and correctly as time and sircumstances will permit of.

Bad news has been brought from there by some of last years emigrants which is very discouraging to some. Not withstanding it is my intention to keep persevering untill all means hope and fortune forsake me. Our wagon is partly loaded and we intend to go tomorrow as far as Mr. J. Elys three miles in the country. Part of the load we expect to get at the point of embarkation. The signs rather indicate falling weather soon.

April 1st — We have been detained by the great quantity of rain that has fallen from starting. Nothing of any importance has occured of interest. If nothing turns up to prevent we will start tomorrow evening. I wrote and mailed a letter to my brother Jno. M. Hinde. the clouds have passed by and we may have clear weather to start in.

April 2nd — We have not got off yet as expected. there has been a constant fall of water ever since eleven o'clock which prevents crossing some of the streams not far from here.

Teams are continually passing by bound for the far distant land of Gold in the far west where the sun seems to go to rest.

April 3rd — Enroute to California. Today has been quite an unpleasant [day][9] but not withstanding we got our things in readiness and left about 2 o'clock and arrived at Mr. Elys in good time. The evening set in quite windy and cool, with rain at short intermissions.

April 7 — Since the date I last made any note upon I have been absent from my book. On the day after our arrival at Mr. Elys I have returned to town and remained there until the present which is Sunday evening. The weather had been so damp that it detained us. however we intend to leave tomorrow if all can be got ready.

April 8 — We made a start this morning from Mr. Elys and crossed the prairie which is twelve miles. the road is very muddy and we made slow progress. We are now in camp near a farm owned by a Mr. White.[10] Miles travel today 14.

April 9 — We decaped[11] this morning from Whites about 7' and arrived at a point fixed upon from this day's travel, which was short and soon performed. The mans name where we stoped was Simpson[12] and in some way related to Dillard Fike[13] on[e] of my partners. We left the Florida road to the right on the account of its being cut up badly by the number that have went that way. The forks of Salt river were in a good fordable state

Mile 10 & 14 = 24

April 10 — This morning we left Mr. Simpsons between 7 and 8

12

o'clock and arrived at Parris[14] the county seat of Monroe County about 10 o'clock which was about 6 six miles from Mr. Simpsons. here we received some information of the bad state of the St. Joseph road Which caused us to take the Glasscow road[15] which is not so badly cut up by travel which is but little on it. We passed on some eight miles to Mr. Grants[16] and encamped for the night.

24 & 14 = 38

April 11th — Early this morning we left Mr. Grant's in the county of Monroe about seven or earlier. The first part of our road was very good with some not so good towards the last. We are now encamped at Mr. Dankins[17] in Randolph county, and are hard pinched to obtain food for our horses and mules.

Miles today   22 & 38 = 60

April 12th — We are now encamped at Mr. Holley's[18] in Howard county some eleven miles from where we encamped last night. the road continues very bad and food very scarce. The weather is cool and very windy. Glascow is twelve miles and if the weather keeps clear we will make an effort to arrive there tomorrow.[19] The cholera is reported to be on the river and we daily meet returning emigrants who thro fear and cowardice are induced to turn back.

Miles today 11 & 60 = 71

April 13th — This morning it was very cold and windy which made it unpleasant traveling. We reached Glascow in the forenoon about eleven o'clock. Left Holleys about seven (7) this morning.

We crossed the Missouri about 5 o'clock and are now encamped on the south side of the river 2 miles from Glascow in the river Bottoms in an old log cabin on the right side of the road.

Traveled today Miles 14 & 71 = 85

April 14 — This has been a cold damp disagreeable day. We left our encampment this morning early and took the Lexington road.[20] After traveling two or three miles on the bottoms we struck a large prairie twenty-five miles across it.

We are now twenty one miles out from our last camp at an Irishman's. the roads are very good considering the time of year and abundance of rain late[l]y fallen. This is the Sabbath and we are compelled to travel on account of obtaining food for our horses and mules. Corn is worth fifty cents per bushel, and hay is not to be had at any price.

13

traveled today miles 21 & 85 = 106

April 15th — I have been pleased at the good roads we have had of late, and should be contented if we could get enough corn for our stock with less trouble. There has been a gradual rais of corn since I left Madisonville. it is now worth one dollar per Bushel and hay one dollar per cwt.

We passed out of Saline county to day into that of Lafayette. This part of the country is thickly settled by rich farmers and has a good soil. We are now encamped at Mr. Beauford's[21] some sixteen miles from Lexington.

Miles Travel 22 & 106 = 128

April 16th — I am nearly worn out this evening, on last evening it commenced raining and still keeps it up, we left our camp last evening and took supper at Mr. Beaufords as we could not cook for ourselves in the rain.

We are now in camp at Mr. Will Shelbys 10 miles from Beaufords and six from Lexington.

Mrs. Beauford is a fine old Lady as the county can boast of and seems to want all comfortable around her, tho her hous was full she made the niggers keep a fire in the kitchen for us to dry ourselves and cook us a good supper. how different would Yankees of the North with as much wealth as she possesses would act so kindly, but few[22]

Miles Travel 10 & 128 = 138

April 17th — This has been a cold damp disagreeable day. The roads are very sloppy and slippery which added much to our disagreeable feelings as well as our poor miles. This portion of the county is not so well improved as what we have passed through, altho we see some beautiful residences and well improved farms as I would desire.

We passed through the suburbs of Lexington today about 9 o'clock and continue on our road some thirteen miles towards Independence.

We are now encamped 28 miles of Independence in site of a residence of some Doctor whose name I can not make out.

Miles Traveled 19½ & 138 = 157½

April 18th — We are now encamped upon a point of a narrow rugged ridge in all its appearance. which I will call the Devil's back bone. We are in sight of the Blue Mills situated on River which is very high at this time. so much so we may be detained sometime. One of our company has crossed over to hunt food and has not yet made his appearance.

14

We are now in Jackson County it is not so well improved in this part as those we last passed through for richness the land can not be beaten and some is very low and wet.

The roads are bad and much cut up teams gone on ahead of us. There are something near one hundred wagons camped in the woods for river to fall. There has been no rain today but a fine prospect of some soon.

The report of cholera at Independence is false so we hear if there was no turn back now.

Miles Traveled 20 & 157½ = 177½

April 19th — I have been laying idle most of the day on the Devils back bone. In the afternoon we made arrangements with Mr. Rice owner of the mill to take our load over in a large five yoke ox wagon. All went off well with the exception of one wagon which came uncoupled and left the hind wheels in the creek, but we soon got them out. We are still in site [*sic*] of our last camp. All our load is in the tent drying. One of the owners of the wagon is unwell and perhaps will turn back. I may buy him out as he proposed it this evening. We are encamped in the bottoms.

April 20th Independence, Mo. — This like all frost days has been cloudy altho we had but little rain. We loaded our wagons and left the mill about 8 o'clock. The roads to Independence were very bad and cut up. the county here is well improved. and the land very rich. But more flat and [word left out] than heretofore. We are now at the place we intend upon staying at some days as we have got provender for our stock which is 8 miles from Independence on the Sante Fe road.

Miles Traveled 14¾ & 177½ = 192¼

April 21st Independence, Mo. — We are still encamped where [we] stopped yesterday. We intend upon going to town tomorrow for our flour and other nesesities [*sic*] if the weath[er] will permit, and one is going ahead after corn.

April 22nd — Today has been assuredly the fa[i]rest day we have had for a week yet quite windy. with all we had some rain. Yet it will do to brag on a fair day compared to the rest.

One of our company took sick today and keep [kept] us from going to town today he talks of going back home.

Fike went on and engaged some oats for us to take along.

We daily came across all kind of conveyances to the Gold region mans invention can produce.

Today I saw two men one with a sack of flour on his back and other with other necessities on their road to California.

April 23rd — Today has changed the appearance of affa[irs] Mr. Hay left today and put all things in my charge with thirty dollars to bear expenses.

I conveyed him to Independence in the wagon today and bot [bought] our flour for the trip which cost me thirteen dollars and fourty five cents.

April 24th — Today we have been making preparations to go off on our way soon as convenient.

The weather has been clear but very cold.

The emigrants are still rooling [rolling] on by great floods and occasionally setteling down arround us until the woods has assumed a living aspect and the hum is keep [kept] up from morning until Night.

April 25th — I went to Independence today to see Mr. Haly[23A] who put me in charge of all interest in team and expidition. Also to act as his agent. he also put Bill a boy he has going on shears [shares] under my charge. We are in all readiness and intend to go to Blue River tomorrow.

I am much disappointed at not hearing from my friends. I directed them to write to St. Joseph and by coming this rout I will miss the opportunity. Emigrants are sill [still] passing on to point locations and procure food. I can form no estimate of the number but it is immens[e] that are on the roads and camped 10 to 15 miles off where ever food can be had.

We are camped 9 miles from Independence on Santa Fee [*sic*] road in sight of Co[24] Grants residence

This portion of the country is well improved. The land is rich and bears a high price from ten to twenty five dollars per acre.

The weather is clear and very windy as well as cool.

April 26th — About 7 o'clock we decamped on our way for the Blue River. On the road we discovered our Hind Axeltree had given away which was in one sence fortunate had it broke when out from all timber we would have been in a nice predicament. Altho broke we took in our food and crossed Blue River and sent back for a new one. Today has been cloudy but no rain until evening after dark. We are now only three miles from the plains and then we leave all settlements.

I will add the nine miles we wer [*sic*] from Independence to this and commence anew.

Miles traveled Today 10 & 9 = 19

We got our axeltree in by 5½ oclock and started by 9 c'clock. We struck the plains in two or three miles traveling. We saw two or three Indians at a distance on their way to trade.

The roads are tolerable good so far. and no rain today but dark cold and windy with distant thunder.

The grass has sent out some little sprouts but not of sufficient quantity to do any good.

We are now in Indian Territory encamped upon the head of Indian Creek ¾ of a mile to the right. This part of the country is somewhat rolling and no timber except what we left behind and what grows upon the margin of all the streams. So far we are in no company all except Mr. Underwoods team which has been in our company since we left Paris.

Miles 10 & 19 = 29

April 28 — I am now on the road so far that it will be out of the question for me to back out. Altho I had no such intention yet from fear something might turn up to prevent.

This is the sabbath but we decamped as usual. We were completely innitiated into the planes [plains] today. The rain and wind seemed to be at war and wet us all through. The roads are very slipery [*sic*] and pull hard. We are now camped on Bull creek a short distance from the forks of the road one to Santa Fee and other to Salt Lake via Forts to California and Oragon [*sic*]

Miles Traveled 20 & 29 = 49

April 29 — Clear as a Whistle cold and windy We arrived on the opposite side of the Wakendau River [24A] about 3 o'clock. While a fishing this evening Perry Smith who once lived in Wabash county came wher I was. he was some what surprised and called me by name I told him he was not right that he certainly did not know me. he hung around but kept his eye on me all the time. after I keep him in suspense sometime told him of the joke. he had in his company Jno Clark and Lewis Higgins of Richland Co. Ill. thes are the first succors I fell in with I could scrape any acquaintance they fill in our company and we have now three wagons in all.

Miles Traveled 15 & 49 = 64

April 30 — We decamped this morning about sunup. The Wakendow

17

flat two or three miles was very bad and decidedly the longest heavy pull we have had. We are now camped on the right of the road at the Cool Springs, five miles from the Kansas River.

The wind is very high raw and cold today. The last part of the road today has been good The character of the country since our decamp from Big Blue has all been prairie except on the margins of the streams whare [*sic*] few shrubs and trees grow, and not enough within two miles to fence ten acres properly.

Miles Traveled 25 & 64 = 89

May 1 — May, I greet thee with pleasure, and well Might I do so, for since our departure we have not so far seen one pleasant day, and vegitation [*sic*] very backward and we hail thee and look to the bright and pleasant prospects you promis[e] us.

On last evening just as I had closed my book a company of Indians came in sight composed of men women and children. They were out upon a hunting expedition. We are within seven or eight miles of Coyl or Kansas River. We learn from some of the Indians today that the Indians upon the other side of the river are in for annoying the emigrants. We have only four wagons in company and will have to wait for some more if we find non[e] on the river. We are camped on the east side of a creek the name unknown to me.

Miles Traveled 25 & 89 = 114

May 2nd — May so far is no better than cold bleaching April. We decamped about 6 o'clock this morning and camped about 3 o'clock on the west side of a small creek the name I know not nor care so little that I will not bother to find out The country here is all Prairie except upon the margin of streams and very little of that The country with large hills and ridges. We crossed Kansas River at the upper ferry[26] they are supplied with good boats.

We passed thro a small village today the inhabitants are chiefly Indians and Half breeds.

Miles Traveled 10 & 114 = 124

May 3rd — May. Alas! for the pleasure we expected are all blasted. The 3d has been cold and rainey.

We are now camped waiting for company before we start out amongst the Pawnees.

May 4th — On the last evening we came across five wagons with six

18

ιιιules and five men to a wagon. we united and proceeded upon our journey. We passed through the Catholic Mission,[27] and arrived at the Vermillion river and there camped. This evening we elected a captain frome Saline Co. Mo. By name of Hays also sergeant[28] We have a guard out tonight for the first time.

Miles 20 & 124 = 144

May 5th — From the Vermillion we started about 6 o'clock and traveled until about 7 o'clock, the first part of the road was bad. The after part good except a great number of raviens [ravines] we had to cross. For the first twenty miles there[28A] there is plenty of wood and water and after that none until we got within a mile and a half of the Big Vermillion. The Banks of this river we had to cordell[29] our wagons down.

We passed four graves along the road that died last year. I had an accident happen to me today while walking at the side of my wagon to keep warm. The mules took fright and ran off. The fore wheel ran over my toe and throwed me down and the hind one ran over my ancle [sic] which had just partially recovered from a severe strain. We camped on the Big Vermillion.

miles 40 & 144 = 184

May 6th — We have not traveled far today, on account of our Mules and the long stretch we had to make from the springs We are now camped upon Blue river We are in the Indian Territory and have to keep a sharp look out. No Indians show themselves.

Miles 10 & 184 = 194

May 7th — On last evening it set in raining and keep [sic] it up all night. also snowed some during the time[30] We crossed the Big Blue river today and traveled some five or six miles and struck camp on the left of the road.[30A]

There is no timber here. We provided at the river No scarcity of wood and water have yet been felt The grass is very backward. I have no idea how far we have traveled today.

Miles 14 & 194 = 208

May 8th — We are camped on the prairie fourteen or fifteen miles from our last camp. We struck the St. Joseph road after we traveled about seven miles, and never have I witnessed such a sight nor ever do I again expect to [see] such another or near its equil [sic] The road was far as the eye could see upon the plains crowed [crowded] thick with wagons in three

19

and four collums [sic] some passing on and some holding in. The road side all along was spoted with Tents wagons and Mules and stock of all kinds.

On our road there has been no suffering or loss of stock but we learn that on the St. Joe's road a great number were lost, as the grass is not so good as on the Independence road.[32] I have to use my own judgement as to the distance we travel.

15 & 208 = 223

May 9th—Early this morning we struck camp amidst all kinds of quarling and cursing. the best of friens here find something to stir their feelings[33] We traveled in the most thronged crowd I ever yet witnessed and all going the same road.

The country is growing more level and wood and water scarcer. Stock is commencing to look a little worse of their use and exposure of the hard weather of late with little or no grass.

We left our company we joined today and are now camped by ourselves. the four wagens that we had when we went with them are yet all together.[34] We are now encamped upon the ridge between the separation ofthe roads[35]

Miles 15 & 223 = 238

May 10th—The road has been thronged all day with emigrants we can not lose sight of wagons for a moment. Altho they begin to thin out. some go fast and some slow so they seperate along gradually. Grass is no better and weather continues very cold.

15 & 238 = 243

May 11—We left our camp on big Sandy about 6 o'clock and traveled along with tolerable good speed and arrived at the Little Blue River at one o'clock in the afternoon. The country is still Prairie. The Little Blue is a beautiful stream the banks are lined with trees, the bottom smooth and even

16 & 243 = 259

May 12th—This is the Sabbath and we are laying by One of the wagons left us today.

The weather is getting warmer. we will leave tomorrow. I wrote home today to CH Constable

May 13th—Early this morning we decamped and traveled up little Blue without crossing it.

We have suddenly struck upon a different climate and atmosphere which has changed to excessive heat, and enormous quantity of dust that almost hid the mules from my sight, and stoped [sic] my breath The road part of the way is rooling [rolling] and high part upon the bank of the Little Blue when we camped We see where trees have been cut for Mules to bark and bud that got out too soon. also dead stock and sick ones that have been left and some wagons[36]

Miles 24 & 259 = 283

Remarks: the last portion of this belongs to the 14th of May

May 14th — We left our camp 6¼ o'clock the road was thronged and dirty. Part of our road was high and rooling and part upon Little Blue When we were camped on Sunday eleven head of horses took the stampede and left for parts unknown, and their owners left afoot.

A sudden change has taken place in the weather. The ground is perfectly baked. The grass is so bad and scarce I fear we will loos [sic] all our stock if we do not have a sudden change.

The Prairie is clear of all kind of weeds or brush I saw some prickly Pear upon the Little Blue which is the only kind of flower I have seen We are now camped upon a branch of Little Blue

Miles 22 & 283 = 305

May 15 — The camp we left was upon a slew [slough][37] four miles from Blue River. two miles this side is another slew, with timber and water. After which we found no timber or water until we arrived at the Plat [Platte][38] river, where we encamped oposite [sic] the Grand Island.[39]

We saw a cow Buffalow killed today for the first time. The roads good but roolling.

I will describe the Plate after I see more of it. one thing I know it is very sandy and the water so thick with it we can hardly swallow it.

Miles 18 & 305 = 313

May 17th[40] — On this day we layed by, and swam our stock over to Grand Island. I wrote two letters one was to my sister Bell and one to friend Ialy.

May 17th — About sunup or so we left our camp on the right of the roads and arrived at the Fort Karney[41] about 10 o'clock here I left my letters[42]

The Fourt [sic] is roughly built of doubies[43] which are made of large mud cakes dryed in the sun The road runs up this river about 150 miles. The grass here is better than we have had back. This is all prairie with no timber, with a tree now and then on the river or an island.

The river is very wide and shallow and full of sand bars, with low banks not exceeding three feet in any place some not more than a foot. the deepest water I have seen yet is three feet, and over a mile wide some places.

Miles 30 & 313 = 343

May 18 — Last evening we camped opposite the foot of an Island which is said to be 17 miles from the Forte.

We left about 6 o'clock this morning and keep up the river. the roads are good but dusty, We have not seen any Indians since we left the tribes of Potowatomie's nor been molested, but they have not let all alone. Some persons that passed the Forte since us learned that some emigrants lost fifty or sixty head of horses and mules, and found them in their possession but they [Indians] refused to give them up and they laid in complaints at the Forte and asked for assistance We are camped on the right of the Road

Miles 25 & 343 = 398[44]

May 19th — We traveled up the river some ten or twelve miles and camped as it was Sunday.

Our road lays between the river and ridg[e] of Hills which runs paralill [parallel] with river at a distance varying from five to ten miles or more. These are the regular plains. The council Bluff road is upon the opposite side. We see teams occasionally as we travel near the river on the other side. A shower of rain passed over on last evening. We camped off to the left next to the Ridge.

12 & 398 = 410

[ff; note he continues with the thirty mile error]

May 20 — At 6 o'clock we were upon our road again we were detained later as we had to Burn Buffalo chips[46] and they were damp

The ridge Begins to look more peaked and looks more like mountains

The road still lays between the hills and river and is very good. We see Large Companies on the opposite side of the river

We are camped upon the river. there is a little wood here

Miles 25 & 410 = 435

May 21 — Our road today layed more on the ridges or Bluff but was good. The Bluff still get higher and rougher than what we have yet passed There is more wood on this side of the river than usual. the Road runs of[f] four or five miles and we have to carry water.

We camped to the right of road about two miles in the Bottom. Back part of the road for miles lay through a region whare [sic] everything had been sweep [swept][45] by the Buffalo and had the appearance of a barn yard and covered thick with dung. We traveled late and had to use buffalo chips

Miles 25 & 435 = 460

May 22nd — We have traveled slow today as the grass is very poor and we had to grais[47] longer.

Some of our company killed a buffalo and we enjoyed the hump and portion of hams We passed some men in distress. they had all of their cattle sweep[48] off by a herd of Buffalo and lef[t] afoot and alone.

I see many ways of traveling, some on foot and with carts and one steer and cow Patched in. We camped to the right on a slew[49] about three miles from the river.

Miles 24 & 460 = 484

May 23d — We wer[e] on our road by 6½ o'clock which lays some distance from the river. we camped about one mile off from the river. no wood is to be had so we us[e] buffalo chips

We hapened [sic] upon a spot that is very good and runs from a half mile wide to two in length and is completely covered with stock Grass has been very scarce. If the road continues like it has back water should be carried for we leave the river for many miles at a time.

Grass has been scears[sic] along the road so we have keep [kept] up traveling and made a long stretch

Miles 27 & 484 = 511

May 24 — We started on our road in better spirits this morning than we have been in for some time on the account of our mules which have been satisfied with grass for their first time

At 9 o'clock after 10 miles travel we came to the Ford we turned out and grazed till about eleven when we hitched up and started across.

The ford is a long one, and covers about ¾ miles after we got across we had a hard long pull up a hill about two miles in length. About 8 miles travel brought us to the Hollow[50] the desent [descent] was difficult. the steepness beat anything I ever saw. wagons undertake to decend [sic]. after we got into the hollow we found the roads very sandy and deep between two hills with cedar trees sattered [scattered] every now and then along the hill side and some others that grew more plentiful. Such a scene as this I always enjoyed We traveled down Ash Hollow about 2 miles and reached the river about sundown, which is the North Fork of the Plate [*sic*] river. The distance from River to river is called 16 miles. We meet some going back and see wagons and camp utinsels cast away and grass so bad seems inclined to be discouraging

We are now out of the Pawnee Nation, Who caused so much alarm and as yet I have not seen one.

We are now in the Crow Indian Nation. We have camped at the foot of Ash Hollow on the River. I will call it Sandy Hollow, as it is a more proper name

Miles 26 & 511 = 537

May 25 — Soon as possible we lft [left] our camp this morning proceeded on our road, but not in as good condition as on yesterday, as we fared very poorly last night after a hard days travel. We traveled about six miles when we came to four or five wigwams on the side of the road which ran along the side of ridge projecting from the Mountain. We were stoped by an Indian who presented us with a paper asking us to contribute some provisions. it set forth the general complaint that the emigrants had burned the grass and scared of[f] the buffalo, so we must give them some food for renumeration. While we were consulting another train came along which attempted to pass.

this the Indian saw and ran in front of the wagon and the team of oxen became frightened and started down the hill, but the driver by his exertion brought them straight. one of the teamsters got after the Indian with his whip and made him jump, and every jump he gave him a lick[51]

We however contributed a little to the squaw and then proceeded upon our way, The day is clear so far. This evening we had quite a storm which blew down the tents and came near upseting the wagons but no rain here.

Miles 10 & 537 = 547

May 26 — This is the sabbath and we are on the road but not from our own will, but from necessity.

We had not proceeded far before we met a gang of indians moving, they had one wagon, and two mules packed in a strange manner to me. The mules had two poles fastened to their sides some twenty feet from the end dragging on the ground. Directly behind the mule the pack was placed. One was a willow case or basket with the poppoosies or children in

24

it.[52] They were going to Ash Hollow where we met the indians yesterday. Soon after we met quite a quantity with mules, and even dogs were packed as I have described, but the men took good care not to incumber themselves.

We proocided [proceeded] and came to a large number who were taking up their wigwams of buffalo skins to move also to Ash Hollow, such a throng of beggars I never saw in all my life. Some wanted provision and some wanted ammunition. We got through the half feed [fed] dogs with no little difficulty, as our mules liked their looks less than we did. There seems to be no end to the number today, as a few miles farther on we came to about seventy-five or more wigwams, through [sic] we had more difficulty, to get the mules by the redskins. We are now camped upon the river near a few seeder [cedar] trees the first bush or tree I have seen for two days. The road is very sandy from Ash Hollow and rough. There is an appearance of a storm.

Miles 24 & 547 = 571

May 27—Last evening we had quite a storm of wind and rain. We decamped about six o'clock this morning. The wind is very high and cold with rain.

The road is very randy [sandy] which makes heavy hauling. We are now camped opposite [*sic*] the Court House[53] this is very much in apperance [sic] like the bublick [public] building from which it takes its name it is about one hundred feet in diameter. We are now in sight of Chimney rock and have been since noon.

Miles 27 & 571 = 598

May 28—About our usual time we were off and came near or opposite the Chimney Rock[54] at noon. This is one of the most peculiar formed of natures works, that I have yet seen. The base of the whole upon the ground is said to be about fifty yds[55] in diameter, and gradually lessens until it comes to where the second bench is formed which looks similar to the foundation of a chimney or fire place from this the column arises. This fire place is about fifteen feet, and the chimney or column some fifty or sixty. It is composed of soft sandstone.

The road continues the same and there is no trees or timber. Ten or twelve miles from chimney rock we filled our kegs, as the road leaves the river here. We traveled a mile or so and camped to the left of the river.[56]

Miles 25 & 598 = 623

May 29—Off soon as possible to get our stock to water, which was a spring (we reached here about noon which flowed plentifully from the hill. There was a smith shop and trading post here, and plenty of wood and water.[56A] We came to Horse Shoe creek about four o'clock and camped, about a mile off to the west. The last few days buffalo nats[57] or flies have been so bad that many suffer from their active appetites. My face has swollen and festered all over, and have a fever from effects of the swollen inflamed face. We have to smear our faces and hands with greece [*sic*] to keep them off.

The hills and noles (knolls) are very much broken up and cut up and at a distance have the appearance of houses, decayed Forts etc. and some like pyramids.[58]

Miles 25 & 623 = 648

May 30—The road continues sandy and heavy, and we make slow headway. We camped to the right of the road on a bench of the hill about three hundred yards from the river. Here we got some cedar wood to make us a fire. We turned out soon on account of the appearance of a storm, but it blew over.

Mile 20 & 648 = 688[59]

May 31—June is almost here and we are making slow progress toward California. We crossed Laramie River to the right of the Fort. Here the Counsil bluff road crosses the river. We camped eight miles west of the Fort. We intend to rest tomorrow. A host of wagons are abandoned here.

Miles 21 & 688 = 709

June 1st—Sabbath and June are both here. This For[t] Laramie is better than Fort Kearny. I have sent a letter to be mailed to my brother and sister. I directed it to Charles T. Hinde. We had some rain today. I have made a mistake and just found it out, today is Saturday.

June 2nd—It was very cool this morning, and the road very wet, which makes it more pleasant traveling. The road is very hilly so much so we put in our riding horses. We camped on a small brook to the left—to the right is a high hill. The river in sight in one place only.[61]

Miles 23 & 709 = 721

June 3d—Three or four miles from camp we passed a fine spring on the right, a good place to camp, road mountainous. Laramie (?) Peak[62] is still in sight, which we saw before we came up to the fort. Today we had such a storm that has never been my lot to witness. We saw it coming like lightning and turned out immediately, we had not more than unhitched

26

before. The hail came driven by a furious wind fretting us and the mules severely. In a few moments the dry and dusty road was running [*sic*] knee deep with ice and water. Good fortune for us was in store as we were within two miles or three miles of a creek where there was wood. Some better cottonwood logs that had been cut the year before was a luxury.

Miles 20 & 721 = 741

June 4th — After our hardship and exposure on yesterday we came off better than I expected. We first passed through a bottom which was covered with water. Three miles brought us to the hills, here commenced our hardships.

We crossed a creek, went about two miles and camped on the right, on the left is a ridge of rocks. Some dead water here.

Miles 30 & 741 = 771

June 5 — No water from the last camp, until we reached a hollow some eight miles, here the road is sandy for two miles. Two miles and we came to (a) fine creek. The road lugs over large hills and we have thrown away everything we can spare.

Today we saw an old man almost on the verge of the grave trotting after an old ox he had packed that looked as if he would drop from fatigue.

Miles 30 & 771 = 801

June 6 — The road now lays up the river which is uneven and sandy, about six miles brought us to the river.

We got to the ferry[63] about four o'clock here we camped and intend to make pack saddles [*sic*] and throw our wagons away.[64] After camping all have gon[e] to work, Hurrah.

Miles 24 & 841 = 825

June 7 — All hands are busly [*sic*] engaged at the pack saddle — work goes fine. It is extremely hot, better than cold. All we could dispose of we sold, but at reduced prices. Our wagon brought ($10) ten dollars. Some things are extremely high, especially food of any kind. Flour is twenty-five cents per lb.

June 8 — About noon commenced the great scatterment of plunder, to select all we could not be deprived of from what had to be abandoned. We crossed the river at the lower ferry[65] then went up the river and camped. The wind high, gave a threatening look above, but no rain.

Miles 2 & 825 = 827

June 9—Sunday has again made its appearance, and we set out to make our first days travel with packs. We have had a long days travel as we could not find any grass, for twenty-five miles from the ferry thare [*sic*] is neither wood nor water, that is fit for any use at all. The water is rendered useless by the alkaline substance in the earth, and the use will destroy the life of the animals.

We reached the springs about dark, and found no grass.[66]

Miles 30 & 827 = 857

June 10—For the last two days our stock has fared poorly. About noon we reached the sweet water a distance of twenty-two miles from the springs. Independence rock[67] is a bold looking mass of stone. It bears the names of numerous persons who are anxious to have their names conspicuous some have seemed to risk their necks, to strive for ascending.

We camped on the Sweet-water and lost from [our company] [Hinde's brackets.]

Miles 30 & 857 = 887

June 11—Early in the morning we packed up and started to overtake our company, we thought they were before, but about noon we found out they were behind.

We stoped [stopped) early in the bitter cotton wood creek. Here we fared like beasts, it rained very hard [four previous words repeated] and we had to take all of it, and the best we could. I have filled this small book. When I commenced it I was sure it would last us through, by luck I got another I have been brief, but punctual considering the great disadvantage I have been put to.

Miles 22 — 887 = 909[68]

June 12th—We are now encamped upon the banks of the Sweet-water. We arrived here about seven o'clock. At noon I discovered in the river a considerable amount of mika [mica] which looked like scales of gold floating in the bottom. From bitter cottenwood to the river is called six miles and then a stretch of nine miles, and another sixteen from river to river, making in all thirty-two miles we have travled today. The roads are very hilly and sandy, with no grass from point to point, Alkeline springs which both of my mules got in and it was so strong that it kept them sore for sometime.

We are within fourty miles of north South Pass. The ridges of mountains are mostly rock, and some snow to be seen.

Miles 32 & 909 = 941

June 13th—The road now lays up the bottom of the Sweet-water and is sandy and uneven. We left the river after noon and looked to the mountains. We traveled fourteen miles and came to the river after crossing two or three creeks. We camped on the right of the road and the creek where we got some willow branches for our mules. No gras[s] here, and stock fares badly.

Miles 25 & 941 = 966

June 14th—Hardships are the profits derived principally from packing. Today we experienced [*sic*] more than we did in the hail storm. The wind has blown a perfect blast, so much so it was with difficulty we got our breath at times.

In the evening it commenced snowing and raining and we were completely drenched and chilled, which continued until dark. We were all wet and had nothing to shelter us, we built us a fire out of wild sage soon as we camped. We are two miles from the Pacific Springs,[70] which are at the South Pass.

Miles 18 & 966 = 984

June 15th—The winds continue very chilly and high. The road is more level and is on a decent [descent] and the water all flows in a different direction. There is no water after we left the springs until we struck the junction of the Salt Lake and Oregon roads.

The distance is twenty six miles, where we found plenty of water, but no grass. We took the Oregon road[71] and intend to go Sutters cutoff we camped on a little creek.

Miles 22 & 984 = 1006

June 16th—Here we are now about the middle of the most[72] (beautiful) month of the year, our friends are enjoying it at home, while we are suffering with cold and chilling winds. We may look all around us and see no manner of vegetation whatever, and not enough of grass to support our mules.

This is our situation in a vast desert, and bearly [*sic*] enough to support life, and our friends surrounded by abundance for the support of man and beast, and still they are not satisfied, and they wish for a change. On yesterday we passed a pile of drift snow 12 or fifteen feet deep and so sollid [*sic*] a horse could walk upon it without leaving a print.

The Rockey Mountains are on continual and gradual ascent and

29

descent, and so gradual that we scearsly (scarcely) notice it. They are covered with a chain of high rocks with mounds scattered about. We see no trees or brush at all. The whole face of the country is barren. The game consists of goats or sheep, bears of both kinds, deer, antelope and Elk, I should like to take one of the sheep horns home as a curiosity.

At four o'clock we left our camp and reached Big Sandy a distance o six miles to get grass and be ready to cross the desert, between Big Sandy and Green River which is said to be thirty-five miles, we soon arrived at Big Sandy but no grass was to be seen.

Miles 6 & 1006 = 1012

June 17th—Last night we concluded to cross the desert or a part of it that night. The wind was very high and chilly when we left our camp. We traveled until eleven o'clock and stopped to wait until morning, as the moon was down and storm-like clouds were rising. After staking our mules out we laid down to expose rather than refresh ourselves. A storm soon came up and covered us over with a sheet of snow while we were asleep. When we uncovered we were chiled [chilled] through with the cold blast of sleet and wind that came in torrents over the plains. We had no wood or fuel of any kind to build a fire so we had to pack our mules and proceed on cold and hungry, and our stock was no better of [*sic*] than we were. About two or three o'clock we reached Green river, where we had to stay to be ferried.[73] Here we could find no grass for our mules. The banks of the river were covered with stock and wagons which gave an appearance of a busy market day in a city where the people had collected. Some were converting their wagons into carts, and some preparing to pack. We went about a mile down the river and camped. The distance across is called fourty-five miles but I will call it fifty for good measure.[73A]

Miles 45 & 1012 = 1057

June 18th—On last evening we had another snow storm. This morning was as clear as a whistle but very cold. We have made arrangements to have our packs taken over at the same time the wagons are going over, so we will not be detained long, but we will have to swim our stock. All turned out very well and we traveled about seventeen miles, one old horse we had along gave out, and set Bill on foot. We camped on a high hill near a small stream. The weather more calm than yesterday.

Miles 17 & 1057 = 1074

June 19th—Soon in the morning we set off, I am now almost on foot

30

myself. My mule has the distemper, and is very weak. We have traveled about fifteen miles today, and are now camped upon the Black Fork[74] where a great number are encamped.

Thank god we see but few ox teams. We have got ahead of them. There is one ahead is all I can hear from.

We can see snow on most of the high peaks which makes the evenings very cool.

Miles 15 & 1074 = 1089

June 20th—The same today as on yesterday, travel and travel and yet a long ways from California. The hills are growing larger the farther we go and the weaker our stock gets the more labor they have to endure. We made a descent today that could not be short of two miles in length. The mosquitoes are worse here than any place I ever saw them in my life. We came to Bear river this afternoon and camped about two miles below the crossing at the foot of the mountain. I've crossed this stream three times. All we enjoy on Bear River is an abundance of mosquitoes.

Miles 20 & 1089 = 1109

June 21st—Today our road layed down Bear, tho' it leaves it and crosses the mountain, and descends again in two miles of the river. Here we camped I am still taking it on foot trying to get my mule in better condition, but alas! He does not improve but grows worse. We passed ten dead oxen today but no teams. We are now amongst the tribe of Snake Indians.

Miles 20 & 1109 = 1129

June 22d—Earlier than usual we started out and traveled until eleven o'clock or thereabouts. We left the road and camped next to the mountains, on a small creek. Here we intend to rest until tomorrow. The mosquitoes are very bad here. More so than I ever saw or heard of. They completely cover our stock and annoy them. I am still on foot as my mule does not improve any and all we have traveled today is twelve or thirteen miles.[75]

Miles 12 & 1129 = 1141

June 23—Sabbath has no restraint upon us, we are out traveling today and can not be blamed much, but most of the emigrants are laying up. The road layed by Bear River for 10 or 12 miles for this place—it left Bear River for about the same distance and struck the river again at Soda Spring this we reached about three o'clock. There are some French and Indians here trading in stock. I swopped my mule to one of them for a pony, which is not much better as it has such a sore back.[76] We took the

31

short cut as the right hand road goes to Fort Hall. The Soda Springs are a grand curiosity. The water boils out of the ground and fills a large basin or pool.

We traveled about four miles and camped.

Miles 24 & 1141 = 1165

June 24—At the forks of the road which is four miles from the Springs a dispute and contention arose amongst the emigrants lik[e] at the junction of the Salt Lake road.[76A] We find the road very rough but [a] number of wagons travel it. We traveled until we came to a creek. The water is very bad. The weather is cool and pleasant.

Miles 30 & 1165 = 1195

June 25—Shortly after crossing the creek we had a hill to climb. The road of late is mountainous. We had plenty of water for ten or twelve miles when we entered a cannion,[77] which was a gradual descent of two or three miles, and only wide enough for a wagon to pass. After we left the creek we did not find any water. So we camped without any on the west of the cannion.

Miles 30 & 1195 = 1225

June 26—Early in the morning we started off in search of water with empty bellys, and parched toungs[78]. About eleven we came to water a distance of 24 miles between creeks. Here we stayed until 2 o'clock then we set off, as we heard the distance to the next water was twenty miles, but this was a mistake as plenty of springs were to be found along the road. We came down another canyon similar to the last one and when halfway down one of our mules pack came off and turned under him. At which he became frightened and ran into two ox teams, which made them run off and caus[ed] a great confusion. We camped on the edg[e] of the road and had no water but made use of snow in place of it.

Miles 35 & 1225 = 1260

June 27th—About noon we came to a creek, the crossing was bad, with slews [sloughs] that ware swampish, we proceed on until we came to another creek and camped. This creek is a handsome one; grass is scarce here and miles back of us. Nights and mornings the weather is very cold in this region. A sign or rain.

Miles 24 & 1260 = 1284

June 28—Our calculation has run short and we have to put ourselves upon allowances. Last year provision was throwed away as two [*sic*] much was laid in but this year all run short. We camped on a small creek upon the right of the road and caught a few fish.

Miles 25 & 1284 = 1309

June 29 — After we left the creek this morning we found it a distance of fifteen miles to any more water.

We camped upon a branch this evening.

Miles 30 & 1309 = 1339

June 30 — This is the Sabbath and we have made a long day's travel. We struck the head of the valley today. The distance to water after leaving the creek is two miles. Camped upon a small river, grass scarse.

Miles 35 & 1339 = 1374

July 1st — This month at last has made its appearance and we are far from our destination. We struck the valley about ten miles from our last camp, and found a creek but poor water and no wood.

We camped at the oposite side of the valley from the road little or no grass to be had, the distance from the creek to the spring is seventeen miles No grass or water between.

Miles 30 & 1374 = 1404

July 2nd — We fell in company with some gentlemen from Missouri and are now traveling with them.

We heard of a man that was shot last night while on his guard by an Indian and will die.

The contry is very disolate and no game of any kind it is inhabited by the Tribe of Root Diggers. We camped upon the Head of the Humbolt[78A]

Miles 30 & 1404 = 1434

July 3d — About six o'clock we shoved out, five or six miles brought us to the ford of the Humbolt or St Marys river as sometimes called. it is bad and mirry [mirey][78A] We camped on the river and had poor grass. The fourth of July is near at hand, and I am in a body of trouble and turmoil, incidents of this day one year[79] are fresh in my memory, pleasant to meditate upon but not so pleasant to forgive. The extream [*sic*] quantity and quality of dust render it excruciating, to man and beast. The Humbolt is very deep and very narrow not more than twenty or thirty yards, its botoms are of an alkaline nature, and swampy.

Miles 32 & 1434 = 1466

July 4th — This great and celebrated day has again rooled [rolled] around and will be remembered by Americans, in whatever situation or country they may be in. The immigrants have shown their respects for the day by a continuel fire of guns and pistols. I had a fine day of it, my horse fell into a slew and mired and fell and wet my pack and I had to go in after him. Some eighteen or twenty miles brought us to where the road leaved the river for a fourteen mile stretch, no water between. The road was hilly, untill we reached the river where it crosses it three times. On yesterday I discovered I had lost all of the money I had, which was about twenty dollars. we camped on the river this evening.

Miles 33 & 1466 = 1499

July 5th — We did not get so early a start as usual this morning. We had another stretch of seventeen,[80] but upon traveling it we found it much longer than reported. There are three or four springs between the river, but very little grass. There is a cutoff from the wagon[81] and we find it much longer.

When we reached the river we found no grass, and had to cross over a mound the road ran for 5 or 6 miles, when it came to the river again. it was a poor place to make a road. On arriving at the river we found grass scarce. Our stock is very tired. We camped on the river without wood or Grass. The country is the same as the rest. A perfect Desert of dust.

Miles 24 & 1499 = 1523

July 6th — got a late start this morning. the roads are dusty. Grass scarce and our provisions short. After leaving the river the road turns in North of N.W. direction and remained so untill we reached a creek, which runs near the mountains on the north side of the river. the road follows up the creek 2 miles to cross it, then runs paralell with it. We camped at a place where a marche [marsh] joins the mountains. Grass still very poor and hard to get tho some good in the swamp.

Miles 23 & 1523 = 1546

July 7th — Another Sabbath. We left our camp early this morning, between daylight and sun up. This morning I made a mistake, and took a strange horse for one of ours, none of us discovered the difference until we stopped and nooned. Grass still very poor. About 2 or 3 o'clock we came across the company that owned the horse and exchanged. Soon after it gave out and we had to leave it.[82] Some of our company came up with a company they formerly traveled with. They were camped about a mile and a half to the left of the road of the creek. here we stopped and camped, with them. here the creek takes a bend and we traveled north and then

34

circle[d] around South West.

Miles 20 & 1546 = 1566

July 8th — After we got up and looked around we found that 5 horses and one mule were lost or stolen. The mule and one of the horses belong to us. Ths loss consequently set us all on foot. After a hopeless search we packed up the remaining animal and started out to catch up with the party we camped with last night.

In about 8 miles travel we came up with them about noon. We found them making preparations to cross the desert, The Sink of the river of Humboldt is said to be 30 miles from here. The Mountains seem to come together and enclose everything in.

The road is more sandy and less dusty than usual. here it shoots of[f] in all direction[s] to grass, and preparations going on every where for crossing the desert. Grass is cut for the trip.

On last evening I passed a new Gn.[83] upon enquiry I found it to be that of Michael Woods of Ralls Co. Mo. I was a little acquainted with him.

Miles 10 & 1566 = 1576

July 9th — We are in fine spirits and in good luck notwithstanding our loss. We have made good time, altho scarce of provisions. We made arrangements with a man named Barnes to use his wagon across the desert. We are now camped in a slew of the river. We got Grass for the trip off a slew running southerly, about ¾ of a mile from the river. We got an early start put our mules onto the wagon of Barnes.[84]

The road runs around a mountain in a N Nw direction to get to a crossing. We were troubled with mud.

Miles 34 & 1576 = 1610

July 10th — At an early hour as possible we started to get to the sink of St. Marys or Humboldt, but we were disappointed. We had been misinformed as to the location. I at the time was impressed we had made. over good time. we were but one out [of] hundreds of Camps fooled. but luck[y] we were fooled for our animals needed the grass, for there is no grass only in the swamp. and we have to wade in and cut it with our knives. We camped on a slew and waded in belly deep to pull a little Grass for our stock.[84]

Miles 25 & 1610 = 1635

July 11th — At the usual time we were on the road in hopes we would reach the "Sink", but again we were disappointed. The road continues very dusty and through a perfect desert.

We feed out all of our hay at noon we cut for the desert. It turned out a good thing we were fooled. This evening we meet some Packers from California and they informed us it was 80 miles to the "Sink" and we had to lay in our grass 20 miles this side.

Oh! the unpleasant [situation?] we are in. Almost out of grub and in a desert

24 & 1635 = 1659

July 12th — We did not get a very early start this morning, as we had to get some grass out of the marche.[85] At noon we got a little more out of the swamp also We camped on the river. Where the road comes to it for water, the banks are steep and bluff. Our horses and mules have to eat willows at night, As it is impossible to find grass. The road still as unpleasant as ever.

Miles 23 & 1659 = 1682

July 13th — Early as convenient we left camp with poor half starved animals. The mules made piteous noise, and the horses neighs for food all night.

At noon we came to a place where some half a dozen companies or so were stopped The[y] made no effort to get food for their stock But we waded into the swamp at hand and cut grass with our knives for our animals, and saved a little for the night. We camped at a spring two miles from the road and within five of the meadow where grass is cut for the desert.

I heard of a man and his wife who are out of provision, and have lost all of their stock except two horses. The woman has to walk. Some companies are killing poor horses and cattle to eat.

Miles 25 & 1682 = 1707

July 14th — Another Sabbath and we are making preparations to cross the desert. We have to wade out a mile and a half in a swamp to cut grass. We have to pack it in on our backs There are upwards to 200 wagons here at the "Sink".[86] four or five beeves were killed today and a general sell and buy of surplus grub. Here is a price currant.

Flour per lb	. . . .	1.00
Meal "	. . . .	1.00
Crackers "	. . . .	1.00

Sugar	"	1.50
Beef	"(dead ox)	.50
Bacon	"	.50

Such is the cost of articles, and no accommodation to buy.

Miles 5 & 1707 = 1712

July 15th — Early this morning we left the swamp, to try and reach the Sink[87] early in the afternoon to be in good time to start across the desert. We left all the Co. behind except Mr. Teass wagon.

We bou[ght] a small wagon of emigrants and put in[88] our mules. We may have to suffer. So[89] [will] our animals as they are poor and fatigued.

About 3 oclock we reached the Sink rested and fed our mules and horses.[90]

The emigrants suffer much, especially those out of provisions and have to push their gaded[91] teams to their utmost indurance. We started out an hour by Sun

Miles 25 & 1712 = 1737

July 16th — The dawn of day found us up and preparing for our trip. We had traveled about 16 miles and stoped to rest our poor teams Alth[ough] we changed teams twice last night our stock appears woried.[92] Troubled and tired we pursued our journey over the desert. Soon as we truck on the sandy road our mules faged[93] and caused us much trouble to urge them on. We got out of water and in the heat of the day, which caused us to suffer.

Men lay along the road given out crying for water and more energetic ones were hurrying along the road carrying out water to their given out companions. Had I not meet a man with water who gave me some I would have suffered severly

We arrived at Carson river between twelve and one oclock. Rested our stock a while and pushed of[f] down the river for grass.

Miles 56 & 1737 = 1793

July 17th — All of us are worried out by fate. We are resting today. We are about 2 miles from where we first struck the river. We are out of Bacon and almost out of flour. Some are entirely out of provisions, and at the Sink" killing their horses and animals. We bought a piece of shoulder of an old worked down ox, and are now drying it in the sun. it is black as a crow. This evening we proceed on our road four or five miles. We got excellent grass.

Miles 5 & 1793 = 1798

July 18th — Early this morning we struck out to cross a desert of fifteen miles, no water. We were about eight miles from where we struck the river first this morning. After crossing the fifteen miles stretch, We got in about 10 o'clock. I saw the river after rising the top of a hill. And never in my life have I beheld a scene so inviting to a fatiqued troop off the plains and deserts. It was well diversified and beautified by a belt of Green trees and brush about half a mile in width. Oh how inviting an asylum from the scorching sun and burning sand. Here we camped and rested our stock. As we have a 26 mile stretch before us. I now enjoy a nave[94] under the first shade tree since I left. How luxurient and pleasant. I have a mind to stay here. We left here about 5½ oclock

Miles 16 & 1798 = 1814

July 19th — Last night about twelve oclock we struck the river again. I walked the whole distance through at a very rappid [*sic*] pace without stopping to rest. I took my blanket off of the pack mule and stoped [*sic*] by myself all night. I arose about sun up and went on to where the rest had stoped. they were at breakfast when I came up to them. It was a scanty allowance consisting of mush made of roasted parched hominy. Also some of the aforementioned dried beef. After breakfast we went on about three miles, till we came to grass and stoped until about 2½ oclock When we started out and made a streatch of 14 miles commencing 3 or 4 miles from where we rested.

Miles 48 & 1814 = 1862

July 20th — We are out of all danger of starving Although myself I am out of money. provisions are brought over the mountains and stationed on the road for sale. Flour is $2 per lb. Sugar $3 Whiskey $2 per pt. We came to a post about 10 o'clock. We seen some men from Georgetown and they offered to pilot us throug[h]. They say we can get through in 3 days As soon as our company were acquainted with the men from Georgetown (a new town just started) we concluded to go throug[h] with them. We routed untill evening to go as far as the pass, where [a]cross it is about 7 miles The[y] reported the Mormon station[95] 10 miles which is only six. When we reached the mountains we camped. on looking at the road we concluded to keep to the old one

Miles 15 & 1862 = 1877

July 21st — With all these inducements we left our pilots and keep on the old road. About 2 or 3 oclock left the beautiful valley of Green grass and took to the mountains. We keep up untill we passed the 7 mile valley and camped

Miles 18 & 1877 = 1895

July 22nd — At the onset we traveled a Mountainous road. It seems to me a man is a fool to undertake to cross these mountains with pack animals let alone wagons. At noon we came to the foot of a tremendous mountain we have to cross, here stoped.

Trading posts are started all along the road. About 3 o'clock we reached the top of the mountain. half of the distance snow lay on the ground. The roads are miserable on the decent [*sic*] of the mountain. I never saw the like of roads. Oh, such bad ones. Dead animals and broken wagons were thickly strewn along the route. A man is a fool to draw a wagon over such roads.

Miles 14 & 1895 = 1913[95A]

July 23rd — Our course still lays over mountains but better road. We have to go slow. Our animals are worn out and grass is scarce.

Miles 20 & 1933 = 1952

July 25 — The road more level and dusty. We took the Hang town or Placer Road. Camped about 3 miles from that town.

Miles 18 & 1952 = 1970

July 26th — Hangtown, Cal[96] 3 miles & 1970 = 1973 according to my guessing. I have been dispirited and preflexed [perplexed] today I have sold the only saleable article I have, a mule for $45 We camped in town. My feelings are hard to portray. The disheartening and discouraging countenances to be met on every hand are enough to give anyone a curious and disponding [despondant] feeling and discourage any strong man. I am now through my long trip but notwithstanding I intend to keep a journal as well as I can. Wages are low and not often to be had, times dull. All of the old miners are loafing.

July 27 — I am resting today and I well need it. My Mess-mates left me today. They are bound for the _____ river.[97] Fike gambled off all he had last night. The weather is excessively hot. The health generally good except some cases of Dysentary. It rages among [at] the emigrants mostly. I am now bothered in mind and perplexed as to what I shall do, here I am a foot and alone.

July 28th — I have been out prospecting today Sunday as it is. No

Sundays are kept here it is every persons day for business. I returned home weary and with no success. This region seems to be dug up. This evening I bought a small bill of Mitchell and Miller and intend to try and mine it a while I feel dispirited and oppressed but not discouraged. Miller was from Chaston[97A] Ill. and related to the man Miller who was killed. he knew Mrs. Constable and treated me kindly.

July 29th — Today I commenced mining with two others. We got a rocker[98] cost us $30. We also bought a tent house off a Yankee. Cost $55. We had a poor days work. Only made $3 or less amongst us. I feel too weak, and debilitated to work. Mr. Foot['s] partner Mr. Miller went to Sacramento today. I sent my name for letters.

July 30 I went to work early this morning to try and make up for the poor days work yesterday. Alas: we fared worse than yesterday. At noon I was taken sick with Dysentary. I remained in bed until Friday 2nd of August.

August 2nd — this evening although I felt very weak I walked to Mr. Miller's Co. store with high expectations of getting a letter. But was disappointed. I have commenced one to my brothers and sisters, but was not able to finish it.

August 3d — I finished my letter and directed it to C.H. Constable. I am still very weak. Can not get out in the day at all.

August 4th — Sunday has again made its appearance. Not like Sabbath in the states. It is a day of business and pleasure. An acquaintance from Mt. Carmel, Ill. by name of Kizer cam[e] to see me. From him I rec'd some news.

August 5th — I am still unable to work and out of money. This is a deplorable situation to be in at home. What is it here in California land of Gold.

I walked to town today and witnessed a crowd of men assembled armed with guns and pistols. Intending to drive off Kanaccas or Sandwich Islanders[99] from their diggings to get them for themselves.[100] Much excitement existed because of the outrage.

August 7th — I commenced work again still feeble and unwell. I made about $4.33 and paid a debt at once. My young partner E.B. Smith is still quite sick. He is from Paris, Mo.

August 8th — Today very poorly and worked very hard. I made only $2.35 which I spent for provisions.

August 9th — Today a friend from Mo. came and worked with us. We done better, made $5. I saw a fight not far from our work. One had a knife and the other a gun. The one that had the gun could not fire but fell his opponent to the earth and nearly killed him. I am sorry to see such fights.[101]

August 10 — I made about $2 this morning and rested the afternoon I was too weak to work. I would love to make enough to pay my doctor bills and leave the place. I finished a letter to my brother and sister this afternoon. I heard another fight in town one man will die.[102]

August 11th — This is the Lord's day and I am the same wicked, unchanged rebel, defying all of God's holy laws. How long will he indure [*sic*] with me? I have not left the tent. The only thing I have to engage with my time is washing, mending, etc. Besides tending on Ed he is still very ill I hope he may be spared to return to his home. He is quite a youth and like myself has let his ambitious restless spirit lead him from a home of much endearment and comforts of life. I feel stronger yet I am closely confined to watch. Ed Kizer came to see me again today, he is lamenting his adventure. I feel quite anxious to hear from home.

[*The following entries were out of context with chronological order of Hinde's diary but will continue as he did.*]

1851

May 20th — I am now perusing this old book. I wrote a letter to Bella my sister at Springfield, Ohio. I would give all I am worth to see her.

Close to this small Book. I here add my first bill of outfit.

Rocker $30 — pan $3 — pick $6 — bowl $1 — sho $8	$48.00
10 lbs. flour $2 — 8 lbs. bacon $2.40 — 6 lbs. sugar $3.75	$8.15
3 lbs. coffee $3 — ½ lbs salt 50¢ — ¼ lb. pepper 40¢	$3.90
2 lbs. salt 50¢ — 1 gallon pick $2 — 6 lbs. apples $3.90	$6.40
	$66.45[103]

1851

San Francisco

October 8th — I am now in the city of San Francisco, Cal. I have been here two weeks or more. I arrived here on the 20th of September, with a small sum of money only sufficient to board me one week. I was fortunate enough to get employment at 50¢ a month.[104] It has been two months since

I wrote in my book during the time I left Hangtown and arrived at Sacramento where I remained until I came here.

I now enjoy tolerable good health and feel thankful for it.

I am along here without a single acquaintance in the city and have to have my own row all alone.

October 9th — I have just finished my work and have a few moments of leisure time. Which I am going hereafter to occupy in filling up this book. I have nothing of any particular character to relate on this occasion. Times are dull and the city crowded with emigrants and many need employment and look in vain. I am still in good health and thankful for it. No news from home yet.

October 26th — I have left a vacancy of 4 days, during wich [*sic*] time I have been laboring under a sever[e] fever and pains in my head. I am now recovering but very weak. Can not write any more at present.

December 8th — It was my intention to keep a daily record of events, but sickness and circumstances prevent.

Providence has been merciful and not cut me off in my sins during my late illness, between the 9th and 26th of Oct.

After my partial recovery I was left penniless and had to find employment. This I got in a restaurant but was discharged not being able to do my work, being so weak.

I next went to work on a boat running between here and Stockton I remained on here until the 15th of November. After which I worked enough to pay my board up to the 30th. Since that time for Shirley and Jackson.

I am now trying to change my mode of life and by the help of my Savior I hope I may. I received a letter from my brother Charles who is in Minnesota, Ter. I mailed my letters to Charles, Bellinda and Martha.

December 15th — I have a few moments of leisure time which I will now occupy in my book. I am still in good health as usual and the same occupation.

I am still striving to become more moral and strict, although often overcome by temptation. I have many trials to encounter, which I hope to overcome by prayer and faith. It is a hard struggle to baffle the many temptations of a new country like California. I am thankful for the many mercies bestowed upon an unworthy.

I wrote a letter to my brother James and mailed it this morning. He resides in Albion, Ill. My whole mind is devested [diverted] on my brother and sister situation. God has promised to protect the orphans is all my consolation.

There happened quite a fire last night on Howsan's pier.[105]

Dec. 22d — I am again admitted to see another Sabbath once more down upon my unworthy head. I am still laboring under the burden of sin. My supplication has not been of sufficient strength. My heart stubborn and unruly. Get by prayer to over come [*sic*] sin and death. I have wrote a letter to my dear sister Bellinda but have not mailed it.

Providence in his kind mercy has stay his hand of affliction [*sic*], and removed the scourge of cholera from amongst us. I have not heard from home as we have had no mail.

Dec. 29th — The City is again all confution[106] and Alarm by wicked alarming us by five fires. I am still at the same place and today closes my first month I have been able to work out sinc[e] I came to California, and very thankful I am for the priviledge. I have not been able to go to church today. I am still engaged in serving the devil, instead of my God. The steamer *Panama* had not got in and so we got no mails yet.

I hear the boys crying papers on the street. She must have come in. I added another letter to be mailed to Mr. Constable Mt. Carmel, Ill., Messres Jackson and Shirely have dissolved co-partnership. I remain with Mr. Jackson I am now about to commence a new month hoping I may be able to work it out.

1851

Jan. 5th — A new year so far on and I am out of work. I would not stand the abuse of old Jackson since Shirley left, and was compelled to quit. I mailed my letters written as above mentioned.

San Jose

Jan. 28th — Here I am peddling candies for a livelyhood. I left San Francisco city last Tuesday night in a sail boat. The weather was very pleasant and consequently had a delightful voyage up the Bay of San Francisco to Embarkadow.[107] The scenery on the Coast was beautiful and picturesque, which I viewed with spyglass during our short voyage.

The voyage was calm and beautiful, consequently our voyage was prolongued [*sic*] arriving on Thursday evening.

I and a passenger started on foot after landing. We felt like walking, the evening being delightful. The distance nine miles. Walking 3 or 4 miles we came across a wagon and road the rest of the way. My night a lod[g]ing cost me a dollar. On Saturday I went up and saw old Mrs. VanArdail who kept Restaurant in San Fran.

On Sunday I violated the sixth com[mandment].

Fed. 9th — Georgetown I left Puebla valley on Sunday 3d inst in company of Andrew Gould from Wabash Co., Ill. We walked to Ernbarkadaio and stayed until next morning. When we took a passage on the steamer *Jinny Lind* for San Francisco. We arrived about four o'clock in the afternoon. I settled up my business and found I lost on my trip.

On Wednesday we took passage on the *New World* for Sacramento. Arrived on Thursday morning the 6th. I went to the post office and received four letters, one from my brother Chas at Min. Ter. and one from sister Bellinda, Springfield, Ohio, with intelligence of my Uncle Charles death and the 4th last from Joseph Miller at Long's Bar Butte Co., Cal., formerly a friend of mine from Mt. Carmel.

We left Sacramento the same day and arrived here on Saturday evening.

Today I rested and wrote a letter to my Sister's cousin Anna at Springfield, Ohio.

March 19th

Feb. 19th — I am not trying to mine. We are on Canyin Creek. 3 or 4 of us are in company. We have cut a race.[108] It snows too much to work. I wrote a letter to Charley at St. Paul.

March 24th

Feb. 24 — The weather is still bad and are disabled from high water. On yesterday we went to Georgetown for provision and I mailed my letter. I am in good health except a bad cold. I am in low circumstances but look for better times.

Mar. 28th — The weather has been very bad since Monday. We could not work any. The rain fell steady and the creek keeps cralling [*sic*] up as if it defies our prospecting.

One thing sure. I will be redused [*sic*] to the poverty of a beggar if something more lucky is not more speedily found. Three long weeks today I have been in expense and not made one cent out of which time we have worked 12 days. During the inclement weather we have been cooped up in the tent, playing a game of cards at times for amusement. We are four in number one a mulatto, and the best friend I have in the country. Our tent is pitched on the bank of the creek, only room to pitch it. The hills rise perpendicularly from each side of the creek. Our tent is a round one with a single pole. A hole in the top for the smoke to go out. We build a fire in the center to keep warm and dry. While I write the snow and rain mixed falls fast. The smoke is very troublesome and nearly blinds me. Unless it quits raining we will have to leave the creek. It runs roaring, and gushing just at the edge of our tent and a few more inches will fetch it into our tent. I can only hope for better times and prosperity. The snow has the ascendancy and falls thick and fast. The pine and spruce trees are green no longer, they have assumed a shrowd of white. It thundered only a short time ago, and in this short space of time we have had a variety of seasons.

April 6th—What to me is the Sixth of April, 1851. Where and how situated I have secretly retreated down the creek and selected a secluded spot to reflect on the day time and position as above asked Seated on the upturned roots of a tree which has fallen across the creek completely hid by the green brush from my companions I give vent to my feelings.

The sun is about an hour and a half high, and has just reached the mountain top, soon to sink behind and enshadow us in the cool shade of evening, seated on the long [l]imb[110] which the creek dashes, sparkling and roaring all other nois[e] and sound are silenced and abrupt and steep the mountains rise on the right and left, covered with pines and trees of living green. This is the only clear day we have had since I last wrote. The sun has come out in all of its brilliance spreading cheerfulness and dispensing delight all around the trees, shrubs and vegetables seen to dance with joy and delight. All nature seems to have attired in rich array for a great and joyful festival after so long and dull spell of endurance, of dismal endurance. Thus the sixth of April, 1851, has opened a glorious bright day dispelling gloom and dispondency of weeks past, so may this memorable day to me, in the bright time of my manhood hense [hence] forward [*sic*] represent the change of my life, and after all the gloom and despondency endured, may a change in my life commence and as the day bursts forth in joy and happiness spread light and delight on all. So may I in the bright; this bright day of my life commence to shed and reflect all such good blessings in its imitation of what life should be. May I commence from this day the 21st years of my existance in performing the good and noble deeds and may all the gloom and endurance forever be forgotten in happiness and prosperity. So may I continue all the days of my life until the clouds of death enshrine me and usher me into the bright and glorious day without end.

All my friends [funds] are exhausted except a few dollars. And the sixth of April 1851 finds me reduced almost to want in a new bustling and wild country. Where wild adventures have flocked from all the world, greedy and avericous [sic] caring for naught but satisfying averice, and return to their homes. Not one friend to take me by the hand and welcome me on my long and much anticipated attainment to all the privileges of manhood. Nor, not a single incident or demonstration to mark the event.

No friends to assist or council me in life to yet be fought. Nothing to commence with, but my own exertions, no inheritance only poverty.

I hope tomorrow we can commence our work and build our dam, and may in illustration of this bright day I be successful.

The sun has sunk deep down beyond the mountains, coolness is spreading around. And so the sixth of April ends. A faint sound comes echoing down the canon, hardly audible. it is my partners calling, and I must go. It is for our scanty supper I suppose they call.

April 13th, Sunday afternoon. — After cleansing my person. (a habit taught in childhood) I have sought out my secret secretary, erected on my birthday, to once more record events, etc.

Last monday I wrot[e] a letter to my Sister Martha detailing my situation etc. with present prospects etc.

We did not get to work last week as I anticipated. The creek did not fall any. It also rained several days.

The weather promises fair, and I do hope we may get to work and realize renumeration for our past labors and lost time.

Yesterday I and Adam Armstrong went to town and laid in provisions. I am now reduced down to five dollars and what unpleasant feelings after so long elapse of time and nothing made. What privation my orphan sister may have to undergo is the greatest disappointment it produces, also it [is] rendering me unable to do my duty and render myself happy by so doing.

After all should the claim we have stuck so close to, prove a failure worse may be looked for.

It is my opinion before I make too [many] more records in this book. We will find what prospect awaits us, if Providence favors us with health and fair weather. Jessy Hendrix left us on Teusday.

April 20th—Sunday Time rools [rolls) on and prospects assume a dull and gloomy prospect. When I last wrote I had some hopes of more favorable weather, but alas: not so.

On Monday and Tuesday, we had clear weather, and went to work at our dam, like heros we built it higher than ever. We spared no evening. On Tuesday night it set in raining, and the creek came up and washed out all of our work. It has continued rising ever since. Today it looks favorable for more rain.

On yesterday I went to Georgetown and spent my last cent. Much disappointed in receiving no letters.

April 27—Once more Providence permits another Sabbath to Rool (rule) over my unworth[y] life. I have just returned from town where for the third time I have heard preaching. And feel more convinced of the necessity of leading a Christian life.

There were about a dozen grown persons an[d] 3 little girls present. Last Saturday we left Cannon creek[111] and camped on the hill near Georgetown, where we are now.

We have no prospect. What may yet be my lot is hard to tell. But I go trusting in Providence. No news since we left Cannon Creek. Fair and beautiful weather. I have abundance of leasure [*sic*] time and will give a short description of the mode of mining.

Prospecting is the preliminary step. Mines must be found. A pick, pan and shovel are requisite. A tramp necessary.[112] Hills climbed, ascents made, winding brushy canyons hollows and ravines[113] traversed over rocks logs and all kinds of obstacles incident to a wild mountainous country. Holes sunk in one ravine, too much tough clay, another tramp maybe to some creek then another place tried too much loos [*sic*] sand no colors[114] and hard bed rock. Thus we go over ravine, hollow and canyons some tore up, looking here and there for some overlooked spot. No opportunity presents itself favorable. At last a strip is found left. Down with the tools and pitch into it. A small prospect of four or five cents to the pan[115] will not pay nor enough ground to induce you to go to the trouble to move to it. Off again up some steep hill an hour's or more, tramping tuging [*sic*] and toiling, then down some hill as steep, slipping sliding and holding to brush until some ravine canyon or creek is reached. A stroll up or down induces us to believe it may do to prospect. A fire is built, a snack of tough bread and pork is taken. a shew [chew] of tobacco or pipe is resorted to. A little conversation as to future luck and prospect. A few remarks of home and its comforts, etc. bright anticipation of future time.

Worried [sic] and fatigued we drop off to sleep on the ground before the fire, rool [roll] and toss about until day once more breaks. Up and out to prospect the new place. Everyone anticipating for better or worse. After the result is known some one knew as much of course. Likely a conclusion is arrived at that it will pay or grub may be made. Then a hurried march is made to our rendezvous which is reached in an excited and tired and hungry state, after climbing and descending hills and hollows. A meal is prepared generally of bread pork and tea or coffee. Sometimes a relish of dried fruit or Bottled pickles. At usual bed time we resort to a dirty lot of blankets [and] rool [roll] up for a nights repose often to lay and ponder over home and events of our younger days. At last sleep deprives us of all conscientousness, until we are aroused by the morning night falling in full upon us. After breakfast blankets, cups, pots etc. are packed up and straped [strapped] up for us to sholder [sic], the Rocker fetched up and likewise it is straped. This all hands sholder then comes the tug-of-war. The same hard and tedious rout[e] is again to be tramped and with a load on our backs. At last worn and tired we reach our new prospect. Spread out our culinary apparatus and proceed at once preparing our meals. Not much is done for accommodation. All anxiety is felt to prove the new diggings and find the hidden treasure. Next is the uncovering and striping [stripping] if near to removed rubish [rubbish] and dirt until such as will pay can be had. Then the rocker is set up where water can be had. The dirt is carried in buckets and washed one at a time. The water washes off the sand dirt and gravel leaving the precious metal lodged behind the rifle bars.

When Sunday comes we proceed to [the] nearest trading posts or towns and lay in our grub, generally consisting of flour, pork, beans, sugar, tea and coffee and if anything is left in company purse, a deck of cards and a bottle of brandy. Here again comes the tug-of-war a man making a pack horse or mule of himself. Such is a slight sketch of the life in the mines.

May 4th Sunday evening. — I have just returned from town. I there meet with my old acquaintance Kizer[116] He reports himself in the same condition as myself. We did not go to church. I wrote a letter to Chas. F. Hinde.

48

We are now working in Canon Creek a mile above our old claim. Tim has left. Adam and myself are working with two other men. Since Friday I made $18 I am not straped, but I was.

May 14th—This evening we quit the claim of the old men. It has given out. We are going back to our old claim I made upwards of seventy dollars up to last Sunday. Since I made only six dollars and six bits.[117]

May 15th—On last Thursday we moved down to our old claim that has been of so much trouble. On Friday we prospected on it, and found it of no account, and gave it up.

This morning it set in raining about daylight, and has kept it up ever since, all the shelter we have is a blanket stretched out on some poles and here we are with the pleasure of providence. Where next I shall bend my steps. Alas: I know not, but a little better off then on last April. Life in all ways var[y]ing. So I leave all to chance and providence, for in myself I can do nothing.

May 26th, Monday—I am now seated on my pack in Shirt Tail Canon,[118] where three of us are camped for the night. We started out prospecting on Thursday morning, and crossed over Otter creek[119] then climed [*sic*] the largest hill I ever climed with a pack consisting of three blankets, one great coat, pick, shovel, axe and two days provision. We reached the Middle Fork of American River and camped. Next day about five o'clock we reached Birds valley.[120] Here we camped, and had a rough hard bed on the side of a hill, after a tiresome march all day. Next morning, we proceeded on our journey to Eldorado Canon, which place we reached and camped. We have had a hard tiresome tramp and all for no purpose. It requires a strong force to work this creek. From our camp proceeded on going up the stream and then took out over the hills, and a more severe task I have never endured. My pack was so tiresome and encumbered my progress. We camped at Baker's stand on the ridge. All of this on a Sunday. We proceeded on our road and crossed Shirt Tail Canon, and from it over into Brushey Canon,[121] and to a certainty it is a brushey one. We proceeded down into Shirt Tail and Camped. Such a route I never have traveled, part of the way we had to wade down the creek the brush were so thick we could not get through.

June 1st—On the following morning of 26th of May. I took my pack and started down the canon by myself. My part concluded to climb the hill and return. About the middle of the day I reached the mouth of the

49

canon, where were two stones. Here I found I had not been in Shirt Tail until now. This morning's tramp has been the most difficult kind. I was tired and wore out. I here fell in with a man named Jacob E. Stafford, as he calls himself and we prospected together, but found nothing. On Thursday, I was taken down with the diereah[122] and remained here Saturday. Next I fell in company with a young man owning a claim 4 miles down the creek, and took leave of Jacob E. Stafford and went down with this young man. On last Wednesday evening I got hold of a Missouri Republican[123] and seen an account of an accident that had befallen Mr. Constable. He had been thrown from a buggy and had his leg broke. I also see he was defeated for circuit Judge. Last evening I suffered extreme pain in my bowels of a severe nature. This is the Sabbath.

June 2d—I have not yet gon[e] to work as my deseas[e] is not removed I intend to commence in the morning if possible. I gathered some of the handsomest flowers I ever saw and pressed them. I will take them home if I am spared. I hope for the best.

June 7th—Up to Wednesday I have been prospecting bank diggings but mad[e] nothing. On Thursday I and Geo. M_____ commenced a Wingdam.[124] We had to work in the water to lay the wall. The water is ice cold. We have our outside wall built. A Company below was doing the same, but failed. The cold water has a powerful effect upon me.

June 12th—On yesterday we finished our wing dam. It has taken a week's hard labor in cold water, and carrying dirt to fill in. Last Sunday we went for provision.

June 15th.—Sunday, on yesterday afternoon we went and laid in our provisions. I have had a severe head and tooth ache caused by working in cold water. We have no prospect in our damed claims, if we make board it is better than I anticipate.

June 25th—On the 17th I was up at the store and wrote a letter to Mr. Crosthwaite. On the 15th moved our camp down to our creek claim. On the 21st I joined in company with five men who have a hose, and intend to work the bed of the creek.[125] Yesterday we put in the Hose. It would not carry all of the water. I anticipate much trouble. On Saturday I wrote to brother Chas. at Minn. Ter.

July 6th—I have just returned from the trading post and settled myself down to rest: as it is Sunday.

I have done tolerable well this week, our company have taken to

$362.50. Seven in number, my share $48.50. Last Sunday I wrote to my brother J.M. Hinde at Maysville, Clay Co., Illinois.

July 8th—On yesterday George Morton (my partner) joined with four men to buy a hose of five breadths at $200. We are to work a claim below. We sold them an interest at 2% each. Last week we took out $300, and only worked half of the week. No news from home.

July 20th, Sunday morning—On last Saturday, the companay I was working our claim with, became discouraged and quit work I came down to our new formed company and commenced operation there. It has not done any good yet. All we have taken out up to this time is one hundred and ten dollars. We have a poor prospect for next week. No news from home.

July 30th Wednesday—Last Sunday I wrote a letter to Chas. HC and detailed my position etc. On the 26th, we took out our hose and sat it in about a fourth of a mile below, we prospected it today and it proved bad. On Monday we took out seventy-five dollars. The four days following four hundred. No news from home.

Aug. 3d Sunday—Another month of this year has passed and another one so far advanced. On last Thursday we took out our hose and set it above the claim below failed. This is about to do so. I have finished a letter today to my friend Miss Emily Crosthwaite of Ralls Co. Mo. I have not made anything lateley. No news from home.

Aug. 10th—The claim last spoken of failed so we took our hose up to our old claim the Tennes boys left. This is about to fail too. I have not heard from home yet, poor luck for me in getting letters. Many of the miners talk of returning to the States soon.

Aug. 17th Sunday—Early last Monday the boys returned from the Trading Post and fetched me a letter from my brother Chas. at St. Paul. All were well. On last Thursday morning we took out three hundred and seventeen dollars, but nothing since.

Aug. 25th.—Since the seventeeth my company have all left, and gone to keeping Ranch, I came up to the store and have not done anything. I fell in company with my old partner of Canon Creek. We are working in company. I am still on Shirt Tail below Brushey Canon. This old partner was named King.[126]

Sept. 2nd—I was away from home on Saturday and Sunday. On Saturday I went on the hill prospecting. We passed through Elizabeth town.[127] On Sunday I went to Yankee Jim's[128] on yesterday we sunk a hole but found no pay. Today Mr. King went to Yankee Jim's and I am alone till he returns.

Sept. 14th—I have just returned from Yankee Jim's, there I met Jim Bonham of Mt. Carmel, Ills. For the last two weeks we have been prospecting on the hill, between this (Shirt Tail Canyon) and Indian Canon,[129] where we will make our winter quarters, provided our prospect proves good. I received a letter from Mt. Carmel from my brother "Mat" he mentions the accident that befell Mr. Constable I read of from the Republican. Our discovery hill is to be called Park's Hill.[130]

Sept. 21—I was down on Shirt Tail today, and brought up my sack. We have struck a prospect sufficient to settle down for the winter and will commence a ditch to fetch water on the hill to the diggings.

I sent for a new book[131] it will be on Shirt Tail tonight. Some time will elaps[e] before I realy[132] anything, as much labor and work has to be spent on a new ditch and preparing the claims.

Oct. 5th Sunday—On last Sunday I and Mr. King bought out a boy with us named Dave. We payed him $160. We will have to borrow money to bear expenses in making our ditch. Today I finished two letters one to CHC and one to Jas BH.[132A] I understand Mr. C moves to Marshall soon. CHC letter was dated 4th July.

Oct. 9th—I have answered my letter to my brother CTH dated July 15th. We are now living in our cabin. We are looking for help to come and help fetch in our ditch. I have sent for a new book. This is full I hope one I sent for will be here tomorrow.

Wednesday 14th of October
1851
Park's Hill, California
Placer County

I now open a new book, which I hope will open with a new era of my life.

The past has been dark and gloomy, with no prospect visible for anything better, but at last the spell seems to be broken for the first time. I begin to see I have cause to hope and count upon better days. I have now a good prospect to keep me employed for months if not a year or so, and anticipated good remuneration.

We have overcome our difficulty in getting help to complete our ditch to fetch water. We have to cut it five miles. We contracted with Beck and Co., they take half of the work. Mr. Russel, an old friend of Mr. King's, has to help. He was not returned from his trip south, we expect him soon with his company.

Oct. 17th—I have just returned from Elizabethtown. I have been working on the ditch two miles above. It is a very heavy job and requires a vast amount of labor.

I find Mr. Russel has not returned to fulfill his promis[e], and the whole burden is still upon us. As it is, it is better for us, as we have made much more favored arrangements than we anticipated and overcome most all impeadments.

I wrote a letter to my sister Bellinda.

Oct. 26th Sunday—I returned last evening from Elizabethtown, to spend the Sabbath at my own quiet Shanty.

On last Monday, Mr. Russel returned and has spent the week in prospecting. We have got along first rate with our ditch. We will have it finished as far as Elizabethtown next week.

I hope next December we will be in full blast, although we have a very annoying claim to open.

Nov. 9th—Two weeks have passed since I have visited my cabin. We have completed our ditch up to Elizabethtown and we have let two miles more out to Parks, Munson and Davis. I now start[ing] to Shirt Tail Canon to make a track for an interest in a flume. Mr. Russel has gon[e] to Georgetown.

Dec. 2nd—Alas! What a breach of time have I let pass between my notes. After I left on the 9th of Nov. I was engaged at work on the ditch between here[133] and Elizabethtown, and I stopped in that place on the 12th a sailor by the name of Richard Goodman working for us was taken ill. I had to attend to him and have taken a fever myself of which I am now just recovering. We have completed our part up to Park and Co. Mr. King is now opening it up at the head. Mr. Russel returned a few days ago he has been ill. On the 12th or 15th I received a letter from my sisters Bellinda and Martha dated on the 12th of September.

Soon as I am able to work I will commence to prepare our claims to work. I hope we are not deceived in our anticipation, and may find plenty of gold. I wrote a letter on the 23rd to my brother J.M.H.[134]

Dec. 7th—I am all alone in my cabin as Mr. R. has gone to

Georgetown and Mr. King is out hunting. Soon we will commence to open our claims and be ready for the water when it comes. I wrote a letter on the 3d to Chas. H.C. at Marshall, Ill. where they have moved. my health is very poor.

Dec. 21st—The Sabbath has almost passed, I have been down to the creek washing my clothes, and have just returned. Mr. R. returned on the 11th with six of his company and our cabin is crowded.

We have to keep them until they put [up] a cabin. I and Mr. King have been cutting a tunnel into our diggings, and Mr. Russel making tom[135] and sluices[136]. I have not heard from home lately. I have wrote six letters to one I received. The weather indicates rain and if we do not get plenty of it, will not get to work much.

Yesterday Mr. King and Munson surveying to Indian Canon[137] for water, which is six miles up. What a pity we did not cut to Indian Canon instead of the one we did.

Dec. 25—Christmas Morning finds me all alone in my cabin. I spent last night by myself. Mr. King cleaning it out. Since last Sunday we have had considerable rain another year is about to terminate and usher me into a new one, with a multitude of sins to account for? My presen[t] affairs are no better in regard to money than last Christmas. No news from my relatives yet they certainly do not care much for me, or they would write. Our claim is not in order yet. It will require two weeks to get it ready for work. Miss E.A.C. does not answer my letters. Friends or foes all have quit writing and cut me.

Friendles[s], moneyles[s], but not wretchedness.

Dec. 28th Sunday—I am seated to write a few words. A new year fast approaching and I am still going behind. The rain furnished a few hours rain, so we set the sluices tempor[ari]ly up and watched out what dirt came out of the prospect hole. it proved all we expected it to be.

January 14h 1852
Sunday

I have just now cleaned up my cabin and rid it of bushels of dirt, and have a leisure time to spend. Another year has advanced so far and I am making my first entry of the New Year. On New Year I was at work on the ditch, trying to coax the water along, it was no good, it is going to be of no service at all to us. And we have gotten into a difficulty with Parks and Co.

they contend they will hold the lower end of the ditch and flume. I fear it will turn out badly, I am hopes a company will fetch Indian Canon up for we are exhausted. Messrs. Hill and Knight talk some of doing it. No news from home.

Jan. 8th Thursday evening—How am I to narrate my good luck. I am in the act of preparing for my departure from California. It is a long looked for event, and at last it has arrived. On last evening I sold my claim for (5) five thousand penneweights[138] of Gold Dust, which is a small sum[139] I think by economy will give me a good start in the world. I will leave for San Francisco tomorrow or next day. Oh! what pleasure I hope to realize in one more meeting with my friends.

Jan. 9th—I am now ready to leave for the city of San Francisco, and am only waiting for letters from some parties at Elizabethtown. So soon as they come if not in a hours time we leave for Yankee Jims. Oh! how impatient and restless I am. At night I can not sleep my mind's constantly contemplating what I may have [to] endure, and the dangers to pass, before I again reach home. By the help of God I hope to overcome all and reach the land where Sabbaths are observed.

The letters I have been waiting for have come and I now bid adieu to my cabin forever.

Feb. 10th—I have for the past two weeks and four days been upon the Ocean much of the time, we have had fair wind. I absorb most of my time in reflection of my new home, future occupation etc, but I have not come to any conclusion. So far all on board have been well except two and they are not dangerous. I now put down a few minutes kept in a small pocket diary since I left my cabin on foot. On Jan. 9th we reached a side road house called the United States house about ten miles on our road.

Jan. 10th—Arrived at Salmon Falls about sunset. We fell in with a wagon and took passage.

Jan. 11th—We arrived at Sacramento about 4 o'clock in the afternoon. It was Sunday and the Theatre was open and I went in Stopped at Union Hotel.

Jan. 12th—Left on the Steamer Senator for San Francisco.[140]

Jan. 13th—Arrived on last evening and put up at the Main Hotel. The boat has gone back and my old partner who has accompanied along to see me safely here has gone back. Poor old fellow shed tears when he left. Oh! God how my heart aches. What a void there seems since. God bless him. I bought me a new pistol for the voyage.

Jan. 14th—I have been promised birth in the cabin of the ship *Brutus*[141] a sail craft bound for Panama and San Juan.

Jan. 15th—This morning I called on Mrs. Bostly an old woman I used to work for who kept the Shakespeare Restaurant.[142]

Jan. 17th—This evening the vessel hauled off from the warf [wharf]. I gave my gold dust in the charge of the Capt. three bags marked as foll [follows] 1-2000cwt 1-1400 do -1-1284 do.

19—Laying out at harbor. Went ashore and[143] stayed all day.

22d—Got out of the Head Gates this afternoon.

23d—Fairly out at sea this afternoon.

25th—Have been seasick ever since, and am still unwell.

6—Today I am a little better of my sea sickness. Saw three fin backs a species of Small Whale. A curiosity for a land lubber. We are making good headway.

27—I still have a headache.

Feb. 1st—Some better we are in Lat. 20° and becalmed.

Feb. 7th—Have had a variety of weather, some fair and some squalls. Also head winds. Yesterday killed a porpos [porpoise]. We are in 1633 NL and 104.26.

Feb. 8th—We are now in a very warm climate.

Feb. 10th—Are in 13.46 N Lat 144.31 E Lon.

Feb. 11th—Weather warm and wind light.

Feb. 23rd—Today we arrived at San Juan Del Sur. All well and no sickness.[144]

Feb. 29th—Left San Juan Del Sur this morning and reached Virgin Bay Lake N. about 12 o'clock. Expenses today $7. Deposited my dust with Vanderbuits Agent.[145]

Mar. 1st—Stopping here for the Steamer expenses $11.50.

Mar. 2—No steamer today. We get plenty of fruit and melons. I let alone all such as strange to me. There is a great variety I know nothing of. Expenses for the day $4.

Mar. 3rd—No steamer expenses $2 Passage $35.

Mar. 4th—No steamer expenses $3

Mar. 5th—No steamer expenses $7.50

Mar. 6th—Steamer came on Expenses $13.75

Mar. 7th—Expenses $2 Steamer left in evening.

Mar. 10th—Steamer could not run. We are down San Juan River in Small boat arrived in evening at San Juan or Greytown.

Mar. 11th—Took passage for New Orleans on[146] the Brig. Globe as no steamer was expected for ten days.[147]

Mar. 30th—Today I arrived about 10 o'clock and got into a devil of a scrape which I will relate soon. Expenses $168.

Mar. 31—I was arrested and put under bonds for $5. Expenses $50.

April 1st and 2nd—My expenses amt. to $27.

April 3rd—My expenses amt. to $39. I found in my pocket the above items and some I have copied to remember some events.[148]

April 4th 1852

New Orleans I arrived in this city on Thursday night March 30th. Early in the morning I allowed myself with a few fellow passengers to be conducted by a lot of runners to a low Hotel called the Commercial Queen. The whole swindling and robbing portion always on the lookout for Californians to prey upon them soon found us out and we were their game. I changed my clothes and washed myself. I came down and deposited my gold dust with the landlord. Until my companions had[149] were all clothed and ready to go out. On the arrival of a lot of Californians — runners are swarming about for clothing houses, shoe stores, jewelers, and all they can. Such courtesy and attention soon sends the rough miners brain all a reeling and he becomes bewildered and allows himself [to be] guide[d] about at their pleasure.

After all parties procured their new apparel and were dressed shaved and ready we procured our dust to go to the mint to have it coined. Now Landlord and all parties began to warn us of all the frauds and danger besetting us in our way, and of the swindle shops open for our special benefit. And suggested us to take cabs employed by the house free of charge that would conduct us over the city safely to the Mint or elsewhere. I was suspicious but my partners thought best we should except[150] so friendly offered. All along up to this time our minds had been constantly and repeatedly familiarized with the information of the mint being out of repairs, and undergoing fixing up & also far behind with work that if we went there we would be delayed on expenses for two or three months. All of which rumors were made to induce us Californians to sell gold dus[t] to brokers who would steal and cheat us in weight. All of the attention and warning of runners only led most of them astray, and the whole put us under charge of the most vile of vagrants. They conducted us to a large house with a sign of U.S. Mint Deposit when upon entering and inquiring if that was the Mint we were told Yes, but the Machinery [*sic*] was under repairs and if we deposited fin [*sic*] coinage weeks of delay would ensure. They offered to buy the dust at high prices and all of my companions having small amounts sold. I was induced to do the same thing rather than be left behind and alone. Also all were anxious to get home and see our friends. I delivered my gold dust over to be weighed and cleaned and stolen for when told of its weight I was minus sixty-six ounces.[152] I demanded full weight refered to the marks on my bags, but no I had to take what they offered, and from this hang[s] a long tale of trouble and loss. Whereby a great deal of good sound information and experience of the world's wicked & corrupt human nature was displayed. It is folly for me to write it all but I suppose I had better do what I have undertaken.

The young man who accompanied me was Petter Killinger professing to be from Virginia. I became acquainted with him on board of the Brutus & Globe. He and I took to our cab and ordered the driver to take us to the Bank of Louisiana as I had been paid in part in those bank notes.[153] We got there and found out what had been done to us [was] a swindle. And refered to the Mint. To be advised by the Head officer. Through Dints[154] and threats we compelled our man to drive us there, and I told Kellinger to stay and keep the cab driver there while I went in and saw the officer. He gave me advice which I will now disclose. I ordered to be driven to the Recorder's office[155] of the first Municipality wher[e] Genors[156] presided. Our driver here gave us the slip when we went in. After I disclosed.[147]

January 3rd, 1876.

M'Carmel, Illinois. This book was layed away before I concluded the end of my scrape. It is too long an lapse and I have moved and wandered over too many wild countries and too many privations, sickness, blasted hopes & prospect, for my memory to replete this narration fully. Suffer to say it ended in lawsuits and convictions of some of the parties. They arrested me for purgery[158] and I sued for damages, got a verdict for $5,000. The lawyer beat me out of it and so ended this adventure. I will now try and copy the remaining books, which were mear[159] notes of the daily passing events. I expected to fill up from memory, but I have delayed too long this job to make it interesting.

I am extremely sorry I have not kept a full diary for 1852 but such is the fact. The trip down the Pacific, its incidents would have been interesting about kitching[160] porpos, sharks etc. Also a description of climate, scenery, animals, mutins, birds, monkeys, fruits, etc. and of the country around Virgin Bay Lake, Nicaragua. My adventures in and around New Orleans trip up & down the river at various times but I can now ony fill up this year with a few small notes I have of different dates & a few comments. Jan 3rd 1876 I find that there are no notes to lay much dependence upon, but will sketch some I find and try and account some little for 1852.

In May 1852, Charles H. Constable a brother-in-law hearing of my difficulties came to New Orleans. He only added to my trouble being an enexorable sponge & spendthrift. He was a good lawyer but from the laws of Louisana could not practice. All my witnesses being bought up and run off I had my cases layed over until full term of court, and I went North with Mr. Constable. We arrived at Marshall[162] sometime about the first of June, which was a terrible cold chilly month up on the Ohio River and north, so cold I suffered. Heavy frost killing the Green shoots & leaves of this spring. After Constable coming to New Oreleans a new source of trouble commenced. He gambled of[f] the only money I had left, which I gave him to pay our passage on the [Raindeer] Steamer up to Louisville. Having sent by Mr. Mitchel money to Evansville to be a position in Branch Bank of Indiana.

Before we arrived at Evansville I explained my predicament, desiring him to take Mr. Constable on up to Louisville and I would come on the next boat, after geting som[e] money out of the Bank & pay our passage, which I thought have been paid. Next morning after I breakfasted I proceeded to the bank. While at the counter Lo & behold I was presented with an order from Mr. C in favor of some commission merchant he met on the Wharf the few moments the boat landed, calling for $100. he borrowed. This was an anoyance as I had been well fleaced allready. Yet I had not the cheek to refuse paying it. But this was not the end. Soon or immediately after I was presented with another order from some Merchant to whom Mr. C had become indebted for groceries when he resided in Mt. Carmel. Whether I paid this or not I forget. My impression [is] I did. (O, how soft I was) Well about 11 o'clock I took S' Louis & Cinncinnatti Packet. Arrived in Louisville next morning found Mr. C. snugly stowed away in one of the best Hotels, (a very Falstaf). We then proceeded to Madison on Ohio River, by boat then by Rail to Indianapolis & to Terre Haut. By stage to Marshall, Ill. All night out in stage going 16 miles. (A gloomy night to me.) Having at last reached what I consider my home, altho I near[164] have seen Marshall, Clark Co. Ill. before, and well for me if I never had, for I never recovered from the fatal condition I got into there. Through Mr. Constables advise I entered into a connection in general country merchandizing with a man by the name of H.E. Ritchie. He with other circumstances reduced me to bankruptcy, from which I never come.[165] I gave up the last penny in the world, and like a ghost it haunted me and drove me from pillar to post. Soon as I endeavored to attempt to go into any business I was hunted down, and was constantly compelled to work under some one else[s] name and direction. I never succeeded in getting a start before I had to hold[166] up to save others. (Harry my son beware of debt, trust no one with your business)[167] After entering into this business about August. I was obliged to leave it to go to Missouri for[168] witness to attend the fall courts at which my suits was pending I will no[w] put in what dates I find until I come to trip to Missouri & N. Orleans.

Marshall, Illinois

July 30 — Sent my Petition into the Masonic Order.
Aug 1 — Richie[169] Left for the East to purchase goods.

St. Louis, Mo.

Oct 21 — Had taken passage on boat at S' Louis for Hannibal Mo. to procure witness for my cases in New Orleans. The boat was laying up for Fog. I am in a state of Frenzy, for I have been delayed in getting off to attend to my suits. The cases were layed over for October, and if my lawyer does not do his duty they may be dismissed. I have been waiting for my brother Charles to come and attend to my business, but he failed to come.

Hannibal, Mo.

Oct. 21 — Night Just above Cincinatti, Mo. arrived at Hanibal at 9 o'clock.
Oct. 22 — Found my witness, Parker & left for St. Louis.
Oct. 24 — I find I arrived at St. Louis. The river was low & but few boats going out. And cannot get off untill Tuesday this being Sunday.

How I fretted and worried you may well imagine. All to no good.

Oct. 29 — Friday is the next note I find and only informs me I am at Cairo, Ill. Boat runs slow, as river is very low and causes us to sound our way along.

Oct. 30 — At Memphis. How I regret I did not note something of this trip.

Oct. 31 — Left Memphis this morning.

Nov. 3d — Arrived in New Orleans. All I find.[170]

Nov. 10 — find the following. One of my cases was set for today. Continued untill next Saturday, as Kahn the principal Defendent forfeited his bond. Capina[171] issued for him.

Nov. 15 — Today the criminal case came off and all hands were convicted, and much to my surprise. Here a strang[e] boy only one witnessed for me, and Surrounded by 50 or 100 fals[e] witnesses who are ready to swear anything and have don[e] so, untill I seen no hope, but Truth at times is stranger than legions of fals[e] witnesses. I was encountered with all kind of false accusations by witnesses & sworn affidavits from parties with whom I never spoke.

These parties had retained some of the foremost intelect of the nation. I had arrayed against me Rosillins Gains Bingamin & others whos names I know not. Some of thes[e] were leaders in the rebellion.[172] I only had one Lawyer, Fields. 'Tis useless to enter into any further detail.

Nov. 16 — All I find is this[173] "Tomorrow my civil suit comes off." This was a suit for 5,000 dollars damage for their bring[ing] a suit last spring against me for purgery [*sic*], to scare me off, or buy me off. This was a fierce fought contest, able Lawyers as the Union could boast of arrayed against me, and hords of fals[e] witnesses but I gained the day. Scarcely an unfledged youth has been the victim of so much villainy. And so many difficulties & dangers to encounter. My life was in jeopardy. Many [a] poor Californian was silently and secretly taken off by these rogues. I can not tell what passed for some time. I remember my brother failed to come home, an[d] my business all in Ritchie's hands, and I could get no money from him. My expenses had been high. My witness board and 2.50 per day to be borne. I paid him off and sent him home.[174]

(Remarks) At last in Jan 1853 I rec'd some money from home. Cholera was bad in N Orleans & I was for a month reduced to a shadow. My life saved by a poor Physican who returned from California. who returned entered into co-partnership with a Drugist at Nashville, who cleaned him out handsomly.[174A] Next fall on my visit to New Orleans, I heard of the poor fellows death, his friends had to bury him.

Jan 12th — I left New Orleans this evening about ½ past four o'clock. (I was very low from a long standing case of chronic Diarrhea.) I met Wm Bartlett on board, from Marshall, he was a chicken merchant. A young man of my gang for whom I formed no favorable opinion. W.W. McDowell was clerk of the "Tub" a nickname for Cincinnati Freighters in thoes [*sic*] times. She was "dead Slow", but Mc persuaded me to come aboard his boat as I was too feeble to take the chances on a regular packet. (Left the collection of my Judgements with my Lawyer.)

Jan. 15th — Three days out and not up as far as Natches.

Jan. 16 — Passed Vickburg 5 o'clock in evening many amusing incidents transpired on this trip. The Cap' a Fat Jolly old chap I thought. But passengers did not like him much.

Jan 20th — Last night passed Memphis.

Jan 23 — 7½ O clock this morning at Evansville as I am in poor health and weak I will see if I can get a boat to Terre Haute.[175]

(Remarks 1876) Then the C & C RR was only finished to Vincennes. Freight was then conveyed on steamboats around up the Wabash River, and boats carried passengers. Jany 1876.

Jany 24 — Arrived at Vincennes this evening 6 o'clock. Left Evansville at 9 o'clock. R.R. fare $1.00.

(Remarks) I found the whole country was froze up, and river too low, accounts for my coming to Vincennes, but Alas my friends had about played out, and I asked Bartlet to splise and get a conveyanc[e][176] but he would not. The roads covered with ice and terrible rough. No hack run the only resource was to take a horse back along with the mail carriers.

Jan 24 — [177] Still at Vinvennes dreading to undertake the trip by horse back, the weather very severe, and the ride will be too severe for me in my condition. I borrowed some money of a Jew by name of Gimble used to sell goods at M Carmel.

Jan 28 — No chance. Left Vincennes on Horseback. reached York. Succeeded in getting a buggy from there up.

Jan 3 1876 — (Remarks) A slight description of my suffering over the rout[e] is out of my power to portray. Suffice it to say I had to be carried to bed, and was put upon feathers, of course, which so effected me I could not move or speak. At last my sister surmised my dificulty and had me placed upon a Matrass[178] of straw. Ever since I left California I could not up to that time accoston[179] myself to soft beds especially feathers. Never shall I forget the misery of this short trip.

The journal continues with interesting family oriented entries but I feel that I have brought forth all data referring to E.C. Hinde's experiences to, among & from the California gold fields as well as the unusual and heart breaking problems that occured upon his return to New Orleans.

It is very likely that I will edit other sections of his diary as time allows for he had many exciting experiences following this phase of his life.

Jerome Peltier

FOOTNOTES

1   H.P. Haley was Edmund's employer in the harness shop at the time of departure.

2   Jno M. (John M. Hinde, brother of the diarist. Identified by Edmund in his diary entry of April 1st, 1850. Edmund wrote under date of July 6, 1851 that he lived in "Maysvill, Clay Co. Ills."

3   Chas. T. Brother of the diarest. E.C. Hinde identifies him in his diary entry dated June 1st. He lived in St. Paul, Minnesota Territory according to Edmund.

4   Bell Hinde, sister of the diarist. He identifies her in his entry of May 17th (16th actually). He also calls her Bella and Bellinda later in entry dated Dec. 8th.

5   Martha is another sister. When Edmund reached California he told about writing a letter to his brothers and sisters in diary entry August 3, 1850. Identification is verified in his entry dated April 13, 1851.

6   Chas. H. a brother-in-law of the diarist. His last name was Constable.

7   Madisonville, Ralls Co., Missouri was at this time the home of E.C . Hinde. If this was present Madison why did they head east to Paris before starting west?

8   It would appear from this diary entry that there was only a weekly mail service in Madisonville in March 1850.

9   Added word "day" which was not present. The word one could also have been under consideration by the diarist.

10   White is unidentified other than we know that he was a farmer known to Hinde.

11   Hinde obviously meant decamped here.

12   Unable to identify who Simpson was.

13   Dillard Fiske—unknown but not to be confused with the community name Fiske situated in the southeastern section of the state.

14   Parris—Paris is on present Route 27. It is presently a farm trading center and was plotted as the county seat of Monroe County in the year 1831. Most of its early population was made up of emigrants from Tennessee and Kentucky. Many farms in the area breed and train fine saddle horses as well as some excellent work horses.

15   Glasgow Road—This route was southwest of Paris and was a logical route to use heading west.

16   Grant's. James A. Pritchard mentions a Mr. Thomas Grant with whom he stayed. It appears that there must have been two Grants—one near Columbus, Missouri and the other near Glasgow, Missouri.

17   Dankins—Unable to locate.

18   Holley's—Unable to locate.

19   Glascow—Glasgow, situated on the banks of the Missouri river in Howard County, was named for James Glasgow, a St. Louis merchant. The town was laid out in 1836. It served as a river port for many years and was quite prominent in the Civil War.

20   Lexington Road—It would seem that a road to Lexington should have been as logical then as it is today because it led to Independence just as it does now.

21   Beauford's must have been close to the present community of Dover, Mo.

22   Although Hinde's writing is very clear and decipherable this incomplete passage doesn't make sense unless the word "do" is added to finish the sentence.

23   Bought.

23A Haly—Mentioned as Mr. Hay in the April 23rd entry.

24   Co. Grant's residence. Does he mean Colonel Grant?

24A James Clyman called it the Wakarusa river and wrote that it was 60 miles out.

25   Another wagon must have joined the party because Hinde's entry of April 29th mentions having three wagons in his group. Hinde calls the Kansas R. the Coyl. He means the Kaw.

26   Papins Ferry near (at) Topeka, Kansas was run by Louis & Joseph Papin according to Matthew Field who described it as a platform floating on three dugout canoes which was poled across the Kansas river.

27   St. Mary's Mission.

28   It looks as though most of the members of the party were dissatisfied with leadership.

28A This was undoubtedly made at Vieux Crossing near the town of Louisville, Kansas. It was named for Louis Vieux, a Pottawatonia Indian chief who sold supplies and services to travelers who needed them. This ford was situated where the banks of the Big Vermillion were gradual. Other places were very steep and slippery.

29   Cordelling was done by attaching ropes to strong parts of the boat and putting men ashore to pull on them thus moving the boat upstream against a strong current. After the sail took over the foreward movement of the craft the men were brought aboard to continue the journey upstream.

30   May 7th was an unseasonable date for a snowfall.

30A Hinde's party crossed at what is known as Independence crossing of the Blue river. Other argonauts described the river as being 300 feet wide and quite difficult to ford despite the fact it was under four feet deep.

31   Hinde guessed how many miles he traveled.

32   Hinde's party seems to have been luckier than most of the argonauts thus far. Perhaps the reason for the large number of emigrants may be attributed to the lateness of good spring weather.

33   In most cases where people were closely confined, as these people were, bickering took place. Many times parties broke up or elected new officers to lead them if they felt that either move was necessary. Sometimes lifelong friendships turned to enmity because of some fancied slight.

34   Evidently the Hinde party is still intact. (Note May 12th entry.)

35   The forks of the St. Joseph and Independence trails.

36   Many people took many weighty luxuries along with them that they should have left behind. The additional weight sometimes killed their stock forcing them to abandon their wagons and disposing of prized treasures. In many cases grass was grazed off along the trail. Hinde seems to have reasoned that some of the argonauts started westward too early in the season and had to feed their stock tree limbs in order to keep them going.

37   A slough is a swamp better described as a place of deep mud or mire.

38   The Platte river is a wide stream that runs very shallow. (Platte in French means flat.) The Oregon trail followed this river for hundreds of miles.

39 The community of Grand Island, Nebraska was built here. Because of its size it was generally mentioned by early travelers in their diaries.

40 Here Hinde means the 16th because he follows it with an entry for the 17th.

41 This fort was named in honor of Stephan Kearney, hero of campaigns in New Mexico and California. It lay on the South bank of the Platte River near present Kearny, Nebraska where it served as a military post from 1848—1871. Giles S. Isham noted that there were "twelve 12 pounders of brass on carriages" for protection of the personnel when he saw it in 1849. *Guide to California and the Mines*, Ye Galleon Press, Fairfield, Washington, 1972. pp. 15.

42 Here Hinde used a hand printer and inserted the words "Fort Karney."

43 Adobe bricks are made of a mixture of alluvial clay, water and straw poured into molds or forms of a size required under given conditions and dried in the sun. They were usually much larger than commercial sized bricks.

44 Hinde added his mileage incorrectly here. It should be 368. However he continued to use his incorrect figure so his final mileage will be thirty miles over the actual amount of the trip.

45 Swept.

46 Buffalo chips were the dried dung of bison. They made a hot fire when completely dry or a smoky fire when damp. They were very valuable contribution to living conditions out on the prairie where wood was virtually impossible to obtain.

47 graze.

48 Here again he means swept.

49 Slough is described earlier in the footnotes.

50 Ash Hollow is a short distance south of Lewellen, Nebraska. It was a well known Oregon Trail area. It is surrounded by rugged, broken country. Wagon ruts may still be seen there. Five years after Hinde passed through Ash Hollow, on Sept. 3, 1855, General Wm. S. Harney led a punitive expedition against the Sioux in which 86 Indians were killed and 70 wounded. It seems to have been directed against them because of the Grattan Massacre which had occured the previous year.

51 The Indians were right in claiming that white emigrants had driven away buffalo, which served in a large manner to feed them. It is not difficult to see why some Indians became violent if they were treated as these people were. The Hinde party handled them properly and humanely.

52 Hinde describes a travois that was used to move Indian belongings as well as carry all four children on top of a load of goods wrapped in a robe or blanket.

53 Court House Rock and Jail House Rock which are close to each other loom above a nearly level rolling country. These two natural curiosities are mentioned by many famous people who each describe them a little differently. Some describe them as castles. The trail which lay about six miles south of the rocks is about five miles south of Bridgeport, Nebraska. The formations lie in the north west quarter of Section 29, T 19 N., R. 50W. of the 6th Principal Meridian in Morrell County, Nebraska.

54 As a traveler proceeds along the Oregon Trail headed in a westerly direction he will see in the distance a spire-like object that soon evolves into the well known natural

67

geological formation called Chimney Rock. It stands about 500 feet above nearby Platte River. Descriptions given by early-day travelers tell the reader that it was much taller than it is at present. It lies about twenty miles away, slightly N.W. of Courthouse Rock. It is composed of Brule clay, interlarded with volcanie ash and Arickaree sandstone, making it a harder substance than the surrounding area and therefore less susceptible to erosion. As a result it has retained its shape for many centuries.

55 Our diarist gives an excellent word picture of Chimney Rock which stands about 3½ miles southwest of Bayard, Nebraska.

56 South bank of the river. This is likely why our diarist does not describe Scott's Bluff.

56A This was very likely Antoine Robideaux's trading post because the old trail veered to the southwest in order to avoid the land mass presented by Scott's Bluff. Some of the travelers were using the new trail through Mitchell's pass but many emigrants were still using the Robideaux Pass Road. F.A. Wislezenus in his excellent journal entitled "A Journey to the Rocky Mountains," (St. Louis, 1912, pp. 64) wrote: We traveled somewhat away from the river toward the left and enjoyed a picturesque landscape... at noon we halted in a little valley where rocks from either side confronted each other at a distance of half a mile. A fresh spring meandered through the valley. We encamped on the hill from which the spring flows...."

57 A species of gnats that had a very virulent sting.

58 It is likely that Hinde was writing about the Scott's Bluff area, a few miles away from Gering, Nebraska.

59 Here Hinde made a twenty mile over-estimation in his mileage for this day's travel. We now have a fifty mile differential in mileage.

60 The reason the Hinde party camped eight miles west of Fort Laramie is likely due to the fact that forage for their animals had all been eaten away closer to the installation. Many wagons were abandoned along the route as well as at this place because the livestock was exhausted and could no longer pull the loads of luxuries that many emigrants insisted on hauling across the plains from their former homes. Fort Laramie was built a short distance from the N. Platte River on the Laramie River about a mile from Fort Platte.

61 Hinde made another error in his mileage calculation here. It should total 732 instead of 721.

62 Likely Laramie Peak.

63 It is likely the Platte crossing at Fort Caspar.

64 It appears from this diary entry and others that follow that Hinde and his fellow travelers made the same mistake so many travelers did, of carrying along many unnecessary items that overloaded their animals, forced them to abandon their wagons and to use them as pack animals to finish the journey.

65 Mormon ferry took wagons across the North Platte river on a raft. Although Hinde makes no mention of cost the 1850 charge according to one emigrant named Lemuel Clarke McKeeby, was $5.00 per wagon. Animals swam across.

66 close to present day Alcova.

67 Independence Rock is one of the most famous landmarks on the Oregon Trail. It

68

was called the Register of the Desert. About eight miles further west lay another famous landmark called Devil's Gate. It is likely the Hinde Party passed through it or near it but Hinde makes no mention of it.

58 Here Hinde explained that he had copied his first book into a larger journal type book from which I am working. Evidently, he disposed of the small original books as he copied the data into the larger journals. He also wrote I "only gave in all of it the general and different locations as I heard them called at that time." He dated his comments March 19th, 1855.

59 Was bitter cottonwood a settlement or a description of a type of tree? The Hinde party during this time was between the Sweetwater river and Beaver creek.

70 Pacific Springs is where the Whitman monument stands in commemoration of the occasion when Marcus Whitman offered religious services there in 1836. It is here that water flows to the east or to the west of the continental divide in a very short area. South pass is so level and gradual that a person traveling along does not know he is crossing the continental divide.

71 Sublette Cutoff.

72 It is likely that the word "beautiful" is missing in the text.

73 Mormon's Ford or Ferry was in the Names Hill area, south of La Barge.

73A About a mile below the confluence of La Barge creek and Green river.

74 Does Hinde mean Blacks Fort or Ham's Fork?

75 Hinde is paralleling the route of present day Route 30N. He passed Montpelier enroute to Soda Springs.

76 Usually trading stock was done by permanent settlers who negotiated with travelers along Oregon Trail and as a rule an animal that was in good condition was traded for two trail-worn ones. Antoine Plante, an early settler of the Spokane Valley near present Spokane, Washington, was known to do this. He made the long trek to southern Idaho and brought back stock that he would rebuild on the fine grasses of his home area and as a result, he had a large herd of horses.

76A The Hinde party took the Hudspeth's cut-off because he does not mention Fort Hall. If he had gone to the Fort he would have mentioned it without doubt.

77 Canyon.

78 Tongues.

78A The Hudspeth, Fort Hall and Salt Lake routes all met at City of Rocks near the southern border of Idaho near Almo. The Hinde party must have passed here while enroute to the headwaters of the Humbolt river. The Hinde party followed the route ably deliniated by F.W. Lander in his 1857-1858 map of a survey entitled Preliminary map of the Central Division Ft. Kearney South Pass and Honey Lake Wagon Road. Other routes are shown also.

78B Lander shows the area having ground springs.

79 The word "ago" seems to be missing from the manuscript.

80 Miles estimated.

81 "Road" seems to be the word Hinde intended to use here. He must have been in Thousand Springs Valley. It would appear that Hinde was going roughly where

highway 80 goes today.

82 It would appear that the Hinde animal was abandoned and not the one returned to its owner.

83 Unable to decipher but manuscript seems to read Gn. could the word be ground — campground?

84 Hitched.

84A 1850 was a high water year in the Humboldt river area. This caused larger swamp areas and as a result forced travelers that year to seek higher ground where they had to walk through deep sand. This situation tired both animals and men with a heavy attrition in stock and sometimes in human life.

85 Marsh.

86 A future diary entry dated July 19th informs us that members of the Hinde party bought some of the dead oxen he listed below.

87 Although Hinde implied in his diary entry dated July 14th that his party was at the sink of the Humboldt he reached it the following day.

88 Hitched.

89 So *may* our animals.

90 When emigrants reached the sink of the St. Mary's or Humboldt river they realized it was truly named because it virtually drained itself into a swamp area, then into the thirsty sand, or it could possibly have been drawn up into the skies by evaporation. They realized that for at least forty miles there would be a "dry" pull.

91 Jaded.

92 Wearied.

93 No doubt when the tired animals felt the added pull that loose sand made on their load they stopped to rest and had to be urged on.

94 The word looks like *nove, nool* or *nave.* Could Hinde have meant a rest or nap?

95 In June 1849 a trader named H.S. Beattie, sent out by Brigham Young built a log stockade and a corral for horses and cattle at the base of the Sierra alongside the Humboldt trail. This trading post soon became the center of a small farming area which soon expanded into neighboring valleys.

Mormon Station — now Genoa, Nevada — is listed as a State Historical Park and Monument site. Mormon Station at the time Hinde got there was in Western Utah Territory newly created by the U.S. Government.

95A Error in mileage should be 1909. Next two entries off too.

96 Placerville, which lies on Highway 50, is about fifty miles slightly northeast of Sacramento, California. It was first known as Old Dry Diggings. It soon became one of the richest areas in the mother lode country. By the time the Civil War began over one hundred million in gold had been mined there which aided materially in victory for the Union during that gigantic struggle. Old Dry Diggings soon drew undesireables who were hanged. In order to eliminate confusion with other towns named Dry Diggings, East Dry Diggings, and New Dry Diggings, it became known as Hangtown Diggings, soon shortened to Hangtown. Old timers continued to use this most descriptive title long after it

was given the more sedate name of Placerville.

97   The word looks like "Yuba."

97A   Hinde probably meant Charleston.

98   The rocker was described as follows: It consisted of a box three to four feet long and about two feet wide and nearly as deep. It had no cover and one end was open. Atop it and covering the back half of the lower box was another closely jointed box with a bottom made of sheet iron with holes punched through it large enough to enable sand and small gravel to drop into the space below. The dirt which had been shoveled into the upper box was washed through the holes into the box or boxes below that had cleats to stop the heavier-than-earth gold. It derived its name rocker or cradle from the fact that the entire machine was built on rockers like a child's cradle. It had a handle to facilitate the rocking motion that moved the water and sand out of the machine, leaving the gold behind. An efficiently handled rocker was usually worked by three men; one to shovel dirt, the second to carry and pour water over the dirt and a third man to rock the "cradle."

99   Kanakas or Sandwich Islanders were natives of the Hawaiian Islands. C.W. Haskins in his book *Argonauts of California* wrote that they came to the south fork of the American River early in the spring of 1859.

100   Claim jumpers.

101   Pistol whipping.

102   Hinde ends this entry with a comment in a different colored ink that reads: See page 109 Diary 1902. The diary he wrote about seems to have been lost.

103   Shovel, Salt and Pickles are all abbreviated.

104   Hinde mentions 50¢ per month salary, but he must have meant 50¢ per day.

105   This must have been one of the many devastating fires that took place during the early years of the gold excitement in San Francisco. It is not to be confused with the fire that occurred in June 1851. See Wm. Bronson, *The Earth Shook, The Sky Burned*, Doubleday & Co., Garden City, N.Y., 1959, pp. 18.

106   Confusion.

107   Edmond Hinde meant the "Embarkadero." The Embarkadero or waterfront is an area presently owned by the State of California which is always lined with ships from all over the world.

108   A millrace is the sluiceway or channel through which a current of water runs.

109   Hinde heads his journal with the dates March 19th and 24th, but continues below with his diary entry beginning with the dates February 19th and 24th. It is difficult to tell which month was intended.

110   A word is missing. I have supplied the word "limb." Perhaps stump might be what he meant.

111   There were four Canyon creeks: one, a tributary of the Middle Fork of the American river; two, a tributary of the North Fork of the Yuba river; three, an important tributary of the Trinity river, northwest of Weaverville and in Placer County a tributary of the North Fork of the American river south of Gold Run. It is my guess that Hinde meant the latter Canyon creek. —Source: Erwin Gudde

EDMUND CAVILEER HINDE

California Gold Camps, University of California Press, Berkeley, 1975.

112   By a tramp Hinde means a search for new territory.
113   Ravines.
114   Color means a trace of gold ore.
115   A gold pan is shaped like a common dinner plate but slightly deeper and is about 18 inches in diameter. It is made of metal. Gravel was shoveled into the pan then the pan was immersed in water and the gravel was swirled around and out of the pan leaving the heavy gold in the bottom of the pan. This operation was continued as long as an area bore fruit.
116   Ed Kizer — a friend of the diarist who has been mentioned several times previously.
117   Six bits is a nickname for 75¢; two bits is 25¢; four bits is 50¢.
118   Shirt Tail Canyon was a neighboring area next to Iowa Hill, in the Forest Hill Divide. A creek that flowed through the Canyon supplied water to Iowa Hill.
119   Unable to locate Otter Creek, but there is the Rubison affluent Middle Fork of the American river that flows into it from the south about 20 miles from the main river.
120   Bird's valley was one mile southwest of Michigan Bluffs. Hinde's wandering at this time seems to be restricted with the east side of the American river between its north and south forks.
121   Baker's Stand lay between Shirt Tail Canyon and Brushy Canyon which was east of Yankee Jim's on the lead between the North and Middle forks of the American river.
122   Diarrhea is an intestinal disorder of the bowels causing abnormal fluid evacuation of feces. Many of the miners were afflicted with this malady because of the bad food they ate.
123   One of the better-known Missouri newspapers.
124   A wing dam could be either a short dam built for narrowing a river channel, or an extension of a dam, usually built at an angle. It would seem from Hinde's description, they were building the first type mentioned.
125   They are doubtless going to do some hydraulic mining. The pressure of the water breaks up the soil of the area being mined.
126   The last sentence must have been an afterthought because it is written in a different colored ink.
127   Elizabethtown was on the Iowa Hill Divide and was likely named for Elizabeth Hill, the owner of a large mine. It was first recorded as Elizabeth. See Erwin Guddle, *California Gold Camps*, pp. 108.
128   Yankee Jim was located three miles west of present-day Forest Hill. Yankee Jim was an Australian, not a Yankee. He was not satisfied to mine as others did, but stole horses to make a living. He kept his ill-gotten equines in a hard-to-find corral. One of his victims located the corral and identified his horse. A search began for Yankee Jim. The posse wanted to hang him but the slippery old professional got away. Later a miner did some prospecting in the corral and struck it rich. Such was the irony of fate. If Yankee Jim would have tried his hand at

honest toil he might have ended a wealthy man. As it is, no one knows what happened to him.

129 See footnote 137.

130 Parks Hill in Placer County was in the Iowa Hill area. Erwin Guddle, *California Gold Camps*, pp. 259.

131 Diary.

132 Word missing. I have supplied the word "realize" which appears to make sense with his text.

132A C.H.C. is Charles H. Constable and Jas. B.H. was still another brother of Edmund.

133 Park Hill.

134 John M. Hinde—brother of the author. See footnote 2.

135 A long tom was a longer rocker. The trough was approximately twelve feet long, two feet wide and one foot deep. The riffle box lay below its lower end and it was here that the cleats held the heavier metal.

136 Sluices.

137 Indian Canyon in Placer County was near Iowa Hill. It was considered by some to be the richest canyon ever found in California.

138 There are twenty pennyweight in one ounce of gold, Troy weight, which means that Hinde sold his claim for 250 ounces of gold Troy weight.

139 Jasper S. Hill a young nineteen year old miner stated in his journal that an ounce of gold was valued at $16.00. Figuring the 250 ounces that Hinde received at $16.00 the total he got for his claim was $4,000.00.

140 Steamer Senator—Capt. Josehp Kellogg owned by Peoples Transportation Co.—Oregon City Route, Oregon, blew up in 1875 while plying between Portland and Oregon City. In 1890 built a small boat 12 by 55 feet which plied in B.C. waters. Burrads Inlet Towing Company.

141 Brutus—only one listed in Lewis and Dryden *Marine History of Pacific North West* was the *American* brig *Brutus* which traded along the Pacific Coast. Reference pp. 12 of above.

142 Nor are they listed in index of book *Eureka—From Cleveland by Ship to California 1849-1850*, Robert Samuel Fletcher.

143 His expenditures for his trip reduced the amount of gold he had when he left California.

144 San Juan Del Sur is situated on the Pacific Ocean side of Nicaragua about midway of Lake Nicaragua.

145 Hinde traveled overland to Virgin Lake Bay on Lake Nicaragua where he waited for transportation.

146 Edmund Hinde crossed the lake then went down the San Juan de Norte River until he reached the Atlantic Ocean where a community of the same name is located.

147 Brig *Globe*—The only *Globe* I was able to locate in Lewis & Dryden's *Marine History of the Pacific North West*, was a ship that plied the Columbia River in 1801 along with many others.

148   In this entry Hinde recapitulates what happened to him during previous diary dates that are cryptic but intriguing.

149   The word "had" makes no sense in this sentence. It should be deleted.

150   Accept.

151   Services.

152   This loss of sixty-six ounces Troy weight meant a cash loss of $1,056.00 to Hinde.

153   The confidence men must have had "tongue in cheek" when they gave Hinde Bank of Louisiana notes.

154   I think he meant "by dint of threats..."

155   "I ordered the driver to drive us to the Recorder's office" would read better.

156   I am unable to translate what Hinde meant.

157   The diary ends abruptly here but an explanation written many years later follows.

158   Perjury.

159   Mere.

160   Catching porpoises.

161   Does Hinde mean mutton or sheep?

162   Marshall, Illinois.

163   Steamer *Reindeer*, Searching through the page of Lewis & Dryden's *Marine History of the Pacific N.W.*, I found three *Reindeer*; one, a brig, hauled merchandise from New York to the Pacific Coast in 1855; another, a schooner, plied San Francisco to Coos Bay, Oregon in 1855; and a third, a whaling bark wrecked in northern waters in 1894. None appear to be the craft he mentions.

164   I think he meant *never* instead of near.

165   Recovered.

166   Hole up.

167   Here Hinde is giving advice to his son Harry through the pages of his diary.

168   As a witness.

169   H.E. Ritchey was Hinde's partner in a general merchandise store.

170   Hinde is probably referring to his notes and at the beginning of his November 10th entry which follows.

171   This is not written clearly, could Hinde have meant that a subpoena was issued?

172   Evidently Hinde meant the Civil War, because I identified Judah P. Benjamin who was considered to be the brains of the Confederacy and who held offices as Attorney General, Secretary of War, and the Secretary of State in the government of the Confederated States of America. I was unable to identify Gaines or Rossillins.

173   Once again he is referring to his notes.

174   Hinde paid the expenses of Parker, his witness, despite his apparent lack of funds. Perhaps he paid him from the money received from the court judgment.

174A   Many people were bilked out of their earnings just as Hinde and the doctor were. It would seem that Hinde was being treated for cholera by this kindly man.

175   These notes made over twenty years after his 1853 experiences update modern

conveniences. Following these remarks he continued his journal entries.
176   Conveyance.
177   Note: The dates for this and the previous entry are January 24.
178   Mattress.
179   Accustom.

BIBLIOGRAPHY

Bronson, Wm. *The Earth Shook, The Sky Burned.* Doubleday and Co., Garden City, N.Y., 1959.

Casler, Melyer. *A Journal Giving the Incidents of a Journey to California in the Summer of 1859.* Ye Galleon Press, Fairfield, Washington, 1969.

Cristy's, Thomas. *Road Across the Plains.* edited by Robert H. Becker; Fred A. Rosenstock, Old West Publishing Company, Denver, Colorado, 1969.

Dana, Julian. *The Sacramento River of Gold.* Farrar and Rinehart, Inc., New York, Toronto, 1939.

Delano, Alonzo. *Across the Plains and Among the Diggings.* New York, Wilson Erickson, Inc. 1936.

Dunlap, Kate. *The Montana Gold Rush Diary of* edited and annotated by S. Lyman Tyler, Fred A. Rosenstock, Old West Publishing Company, Denver, Colorado and the University of Utah Press, Salt Lake City, Utah, 1969.

Eno, Henry. *Twenty Years on the Pacifid Slope — Letters of Henry Eno from California and Nevada 1848-1871.* Edited and with an Introduction by W. Turrentine Jackson, New Haven & London, Yale University Press, 1965.

Ferguson, Charles D. *The Experiences of a Forty-niner.* Cleveland, Ohio. The Williams Publishing Co., 1888.

Fletcher, Robert Samuel. *Eureka — From Cleveland by Ship to California — 1849-1850.*

Gerstacker's Travels Translated from the German of Frederick Gerstacker, London, T. Nelson and Sons, Paternoster Row and Edinburgh, 1854.

Gray, Charles Glass. *The Overland Journal of.* Edited with an Introduction by Thomas D. Clark Huntington Library, San Marino, California, 1976.

Gudde, Erwin. *California Gold Camps,* University of California Press, Berkeley, 1975. Kindly furnished by the California Historical Society, San Francisco, California.

Hadley, Virginia. *Guide to the Mother Lode Country.* Automobile Club of Southern California, 1967.

Hannon, Jessie Gould. *The Boston-Newton Company Venture From Massachusetts to California in 1849.* University of Nebraska Press, Lincoln, (1969).

Haskins, C.W. *Argonauts of California.* Published for the author by Fords, Howard and Hulbert, New York, 1890.

Howe, Octavius Thorndike. *Argonauts of '49.* Cambridge, Harvard University Press, 1923.

Jackson, Joseph Henry. (Editor-in-Chief). *Gold Rush Album.* Charles Scribner's Sons, New York, 1949.

Jenkins, Olaf P., (Editor). *The Mother Lode Country,* (Centennial Ed.) Geologic Guidebook, Along Highway 49. Sierran Gold Belt. San Francisco Bulletin No. 141., Sept. 1948.

Johnson, Paul C. *Pictorial History of California.* Bonanza Books, New York, (1970).

Lewis & Dryden. *Marine History of the Pacific Northwest.* Portland, Oregon, 1895.

Martin, Cy and Jeannie. *Gold and Where They Found It.* Trans-Anglo Books, (Corona del Mar, California), (1974).

Myrick, Thomas S. *Letters of Thomas S. Myrick from California to the Jackson Michigan, American Citizen 1849-1855.* The Cumming Press, Mount Pleasant, Michigan, (1971).

Nunis, Doyce B. (Jr.), (edited with introduction and notes by). *The Letters of a Young Miner.* John Howell Books, San Francisco, 1964.

Paul, Rodman W. *California Gold.* Harvard University Press, Cambridge, 1947.

Quaife, Milo Milton, (Editor). *Pictures of Gold Rush California.* The Citadel Press, New York, (1967).

Read, George Willis (1819-1880). *A Pioneer of 1850.* Edited by Georgia Willis Read, Little Brown and Company, Boston, 1927.

Robinson, Alfred. *Life in California and Chinigchinich.* by Friar Geronimo Boscana, Peregrine Publishers, Inc., Santa Barbara & Salt Lake City, 1970.

Royce, Sarah. *A Frontier Lady*. Edited by Ralph Henry Gabriel, University of Nebraska Press, Lincoln & London, 1932, 1960.

Strong, Phil. *Gold In Them Hills*. Doubleday & Company, Inc. Garden City, New York, 1957.

Sutter's Fort, State Historical Monument. Distributed by Dept. of General Services, Document Division, P.O. Box 20190, Sacramento, California 95820, (n.d.).

Taylor, William. *California Life Illustrated*. New York, Published for the author by Carlton & Porter, 200 Mulberry Street, 1859.

Wells, Evelyn and Peterson, Harry C. *The 49ers*. Doubleday & Co., Inc., Garden City, N.Y., 1949.

Weston, Otheto. *Mother Lode Album*. Stanford University Press, 1948.

Wheat, Carl I. *Mapping the Transmississippi West*. Institute of Historical Cartography, Burlingame, California, 1957-1963. (Five vols. in six).

Wislizenus, F.A. *A Journey to the Rocky Mountains*. Missouri Historical Society, St. Louis, 1912.

Wright, E.W. (Editor). *Lewis and Dryden's Marine History of the Pacific Northwest*. Portland, Oregon, 1895.

MAPS

Lander, F.W. Preliminary map of the Central Division Fort Kearney South Pass and Honey Lake Wagon Road 1857-1858.

Wheat, Carl I. *Mapping the Transmississippi West*. (Five vols. in 6). Institute of Historical Cartography, Burlingame, California 1957-1863.

Index

W

Y

COLOPHON

The Jerome Peltier JOURNAL OF EDMUND CAVILEER HINDE was printed in the workshop of Glen Adams, which is located in the sleepy country village of Fairfield, southern Spokane County, Washington State. The book was set in type by Dale La Tendresse, using a 7300 Editwriter computer photosetter. The text is 12 point Baskerville, and page numbers are twelve point Baskerville Bold. Camera-darkroom work is by Evelyn Foote Clausen, using a VIC NuArc camera. The film was stripped, opaqued and plates made by Dale La Tendresse. The sheets were printed by Bob La Tendresse using a 28-inch Heidelberg press. The printed sheets were folded by Millie Ferger, using an air-operated Baum folding machine, and then assembled into books. The paper stock is sixty pound Simpson Opaque. We had no particular difficulty with the work.